quick-method
LIBERTY QUILTS

A LEISURE ARTS PUBLICATION
PRESENTED BY OXMOOR HOUSE

EDITORIAL STAFF

Vice President and Editor-in-Chief:
  Anne Van Wagner Childs
Executive Director: Sandra Graham Case
Editorial Director: Susan Frantz Wiles
Publications Director: Carla Bentley
Creative Art Director: Gloria Bearden
Production Art Director: Melinda Stout

DESIGN
Design Director:
  Patricia Wallenfang Sowers
Senior Designer: Linda Diehl Tiano

PRODUCTION
Managing Editor: Sherry Taylor O'Connor
Technical Writers: Sherry Solida Ford,
  Kathleen Coughran Magee, and
  Barbara McClintock Vechik

EDITORIAL
Managing Editor: Linda L. Trimble
Associate Editor: Terri Leming Davidson
Assistant Editors:
  Tammi Williamson Bradley,
  Robyn Sheffield-Edwards, and
  Darla Burdette Kelsay
Copy Editor: Laura Lee Weland

ART
Book/Magazine Art Director:
  Diane M. Hugo
Senior Production Artist:
  M. Katherine Yancey
Photography Stylists: Christina Tiano Myers,
  Karen Smart Hall, and Aurora Huston

BUSINESS STAFF

Publisher: Bruce Akin
Vice President, Finance: Tom Siebenmorgen
Vice President, Retail Sales:
  Thomas L. Carlisle
Retail Sales Director: Richard Tignor
Vice President, Retail Marketing:
  Pam Stebbins
Retail Marketing Director:
  Margaret Sweetin
Retail Customer Services Manager:
  Carolyn Pruss

General Merchandise Manager:
  Russ Barnett
Distribution Director: Ed M. Strackbein
Vice President, Marketing:
  Guy A. Crossley
Marketing Manager: Byron L. Taylor
Print Production Manager: Laura Lockhart
Print Production Coordinator:
  Nancy Reddick Baker

Library of Congress Catalog Number 96-76036
Hardcover ISBN 0-8487-1565-9
Softcover ISBN 1-57486-020-8

INTRODUCTION

"Make quilts — save the blankets for our boys over there!" was the home-front cry during World War I. *And quilters rallied to the cause, dutifully renewing an Early American tradition of patriotic patchwork known as liberty quilts. Such love of country is a trademark of American quilters, who have always found time to create a little comfort, whether for a faraway soldier or for their own pioneer families. In salute to that devotion, we present* Quick-Method Liberty Quilts. *This all-American parade of patchwork is pieced in shades of red, white, and blue using the best of today's timesaving methods. You'll use the latest tools and techniques to quickly and accurately piece your own heirloom projects — and you'll even discover ways to simplify templates and appliqués! Whether you've just begun to quilt or you've been at it for years, you'll be delighted by a spectacular array of designs. Each flag-waving quilt and wall hanging is rated by skill level, so you'll know exactly which projects are right for you. There's also a battery of smaller, fast-to-stitch items such as pillows, window treatments, decorated clothing, and a table runner. So turn the page and begin celebrating the freedom you'll find by quilting the quick-method way!*

TABLE OF CONTENTS

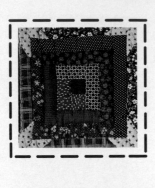
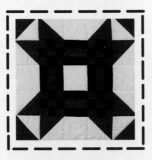

STARRY LOG CABIN COLLECTION

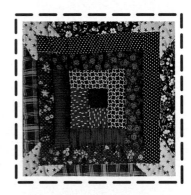

A hallmark of pioneer America, the log cabin became a symbol of the ingenuity and perseverance that forged the foundation for a young nation. Naturally, it also inspired one of the earliest — and most enduring — quilt patterns. Created with a medley of old-fashioned print fabrics, our Starry Log Cabin quilt captures the essence of life on the prairie beneath an open sky. Always loved for its simple construction, the pattern is created by stitching the "logs" around a center square and then trimming them to size. To make it even easier, we show you how to use a template with your rotary cutting ruler so you can work in the LeMoyne Stars as you go!

Stitch a few extra blocks from the Starry Log Cabin quilt and use them to create this handsome wall hanging (opposite). It's completed with a dark blue calico border for a dramatic accent. Coordinating throw pillows (below) will complete the bedroom in star-spangled style. Each pillow is created with four simple quilt blocks and finished with welted trim.

STARRY LOG CABIN QUILT

SKILL LEVEL: 1 2 3 4 5
BLOCK SIZE: 9" x 9"
QUILT SIZE: 88" x 106"

YARDAGE REQUIREMENTS
Yardage is based on 45"w fabric.

- 4½ yds *total* of assorted blue prints
- 4 yds *total* of assorted red prints
- 3⅜ yds of floral print for borders
- 1 yd *each* of tan/red print and tan/blue print
- ¼ yd of dark red solid
  8 yds for backing
  1 yd for binding
  120" x 120" batting

You will also need:
  tracing paper
  transparent tape

CUTTING OUT THE PIECES
All measurements include a ¼" seam allowance. Follow
***Rotary Cutting**, page 144, to cut fabric.*

1. **From assorted blue prints:**
   - Cut a total of 90 **strips** 1½"w.

2. **From assorted red prints:**
   - Cut a total of 80 **strips** 1½"w.

3. **From floral print for borders:**
   - Cut 2 lengthwise **side borders** 8" x 109".
   - Cut 2 lengthwise **top/bottom borders** 8" x 92".

4. **From tan/red and tan/blue print:**
   - Cut 18 **strips** 1½"w from *each* fabric.

5. **From dark red solid:**
   - Cut 3 strips 1½"w. From these strips, cut 80
     squares 1½" x 1½".

ASSEMBLING THE QUILT TOP
*Follow **Piecing and Pressing**, page 146, to make quilt top.*

1. Referring to **Fig. 1**, align 45° marking (shown in
   pink) on ruler with lower edge of 1 tan/blue
   print **strip**. Cut along right edge of ruler to cut
   1 end of **strip** at a 45° angle.

Fig. 1

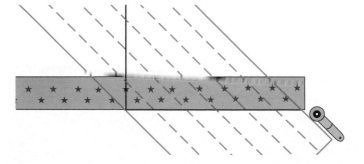

2. Turn cut **strip** 180° on mat and align 45°
   marking on ruler with lower edge of **strip**. Align
   the previously cut 45° edge with 1½" marking
   on ruler. Cut **strip** at 1½" intervals as shown in
   Fig. 2 to cut **diamonds**.

Fig. 2

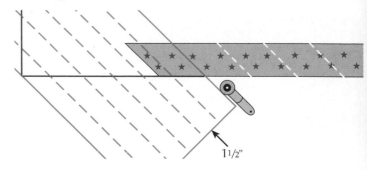

1½"

3. Using remaining tan print **strips**, repeat Steps 1
   and 2 to cut a total of 320 **diamond A's** from
   tan/blue print and 320 **diamond B's** from
   tan/red print.

diamond A (cut 320)   **diamond B** (cut 320)

4. To make paper template, carefully trace Trapezoid
   pattern, page 15, onto tracing paper; cut out on
   solid line. Use transparent tape to securely tape
   template to **wrong** side of ruler, aligning diagonal
   template edges with ruler edges (**Fig. 3**).

Fig. 3

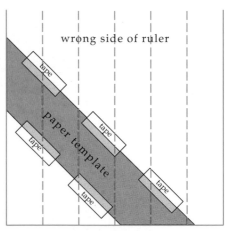

wrong side of ruler
tape
paper template
tape
tape
tape

5. Place ruler template side down on 1 red print
   strip, aligning long edges of template with long
   edges of strip. Cut along both edges of ruler to
   cut 1 **trapezoid** (**Fig. 4a**).

Fig. 4a

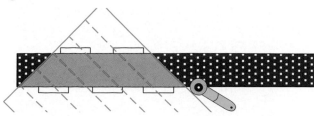

6. Turn ruler 180° and align template edges with **strip** edges to cut another **trapezoid** (**Fig. 4b**). Turning ruler after each cut, cut 6 **trapezoids** from **strip**.

Fig. 4b

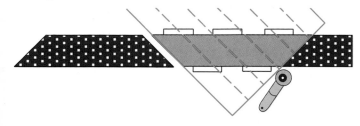

7. Using red print and blue print **strips**, repeat Steps 5 and 6 to cut a total of 160 **red trapezoids** and 160 **blue trapezoids**. (You will need 2 matching **red** and 2 matching **blue trapezoids** for each of 80 Blocks.)

red trapezoid (cut 160)

blue trapezoid (cut 160)

8. Sew 1 **diamond A** to left end and 1 **diamond B** to right end of 1 **red trapezoid** to make **Unit 1**. Make 160 **Unit 1's**.

Unit 1 (make 160)

9. Sew 1 **diamond A** to left end and 1 **diamond B** to right end of 1 **blue trapezoid** to make **Unit 2**. Make 160 **Unit 2's**.

Unit 2 (make 160)

10. Place 1 red print **strip** on 1 **square** with right sides together and raw edges matching. Stitch as shown in **Fig. 5a**. Trim strip even with square (**Fig. 5b**); press open (**Fig. 5c**).

Fig. 5a   **Fig. 5b**   **Fig. 5c**

11. Turn **square** ¼ turn to the left. Using same red print strip, repeat Step 10 to add the next "log" as shown in **Figs. 6a - 6c**.

Fig. 6a   **Fig. 6b**   **Fig. 6c**

12. Repeat Step 11, adding 2 matching blue print logs to remaining 2 sides of **square** (**Fig. 7**).

Fig. 7

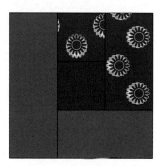

13. Continue adding **strips**, alternating 2 matching red print strips and 2 matching blue print strips until there are 3 logs on each side of square to make **Unit 3**.

Unit 3

14. Repeat Steps 10 - 13 to make 80 **Unit 3's**.
15. (*Note:* Follow Steps 15 - 17 to make 80 Blocks.) Beginning and ending stitching exactly ¼" from edges of Unit 3 and backstitching at each end, sew 1 **Unit 1** to 1 **Unit 3** (**Fig. 8**).

Fig. 8

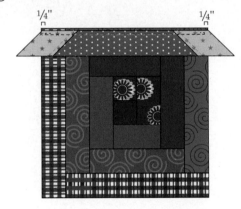

16. Repeat Step 15 to sew a matching **Unit 1**, then 2 matching **Unit 2's** to **Unit 3**, matching red trapezoids to red logs and blue trapezoids to blue logs.
17. To complete stitching at corners, fold 2 adjacent **diamonds** with right sides together and stitch from end of previous stitching to outside edge, backstitching at beginning of seam (**Fig. 9**). Repeat for remaining corners to complete **Block**.

Fig. 9

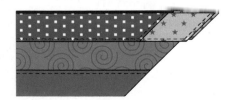

14

Block (make 80)

18. Sew 8 **Blocks** together to make **Row**. Make 10 **Rows**.

Row (make 10)

19. Referring to **Quilt Top Diagram**, sew **Rows** together to make center section of quilt top.
20. Follow **Adding Mitered Borders**, page 151, to sew **borders** to center section to complete **Quilt Top**.

COMPLETING THE QUILT
1. Follow **Quilting**, page 151, to mark, layer, and quilt using **Quilting Diagram** as a suggestion. Our quilt is hand quilted.
2. Cut a 32" square of binding fabric. Follow **Binding**, page 155, to bind quilt using 2½"w bias binding with mitered corners.

Quilt Top Diagram

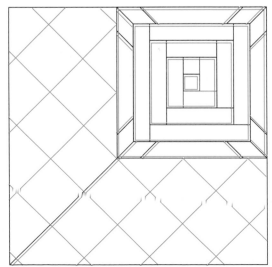

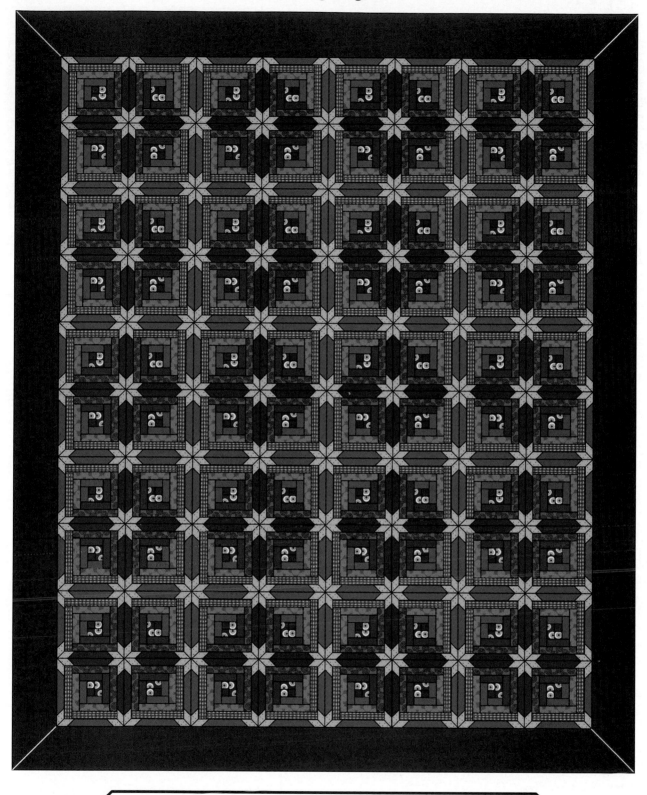

Trapezoid

THROW PILLOW

BLOCK SIZE: 9" x 9"
PILLOW SIZE: 19" x 19"

Instructions are for making 1 pillow. While our diagram shows a pillow with blue "logs" at the center, you can easily change the look of your pillow by turning the same blocks so the red logs are at the center.

SUPPLIES

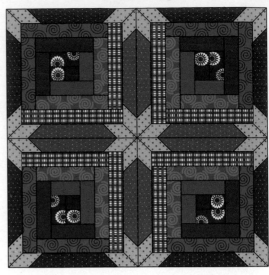

Pillow Top

■ scraps of assorted red print and blue print fabrics
⊞ scraps of tan/blue print and tan/red print fabrics
■ scrap of dark red solid fabric
22" x 22" square of fabric for backing
5/8 yd of 45"w fabric for pillow back
22" x 22" batting
polyester fiberfill
2¹/2 yds of 2"w bias fabric strip for welting
2¹/2 yds of ¹/4" cord for welting

MAKING THE PILLOW

All measurements include a ¹/4" seam allowance. Follow Rotary Cutting, page 144, and Piecing and Pressing, page 146, to make pillow.

1. Cut tan/blue and tan/red print scraps into 1¹/2"w **strips**. Follow Steps 1 - 3 of **Assembling the Quilt Top**, page 12, to cut 16 **diamond A's** and 16 **diamond B's**.
2. Cut 4 assorted **strips** 1¹/2" x 15" from red print scraps. Repeat for blue print scraps. Follow Steps 4 - 7 of **Assembling the Quilt Top**, page 12, to cut 2 **trapezoids** from each **strip**. (You will need 2 matching **red** and 2 matching **blue trapezoids** for each of 4 Blocks.)
3. Follow Steps 8 and 9 of **Assembling the Quilt Top**, page 13, to make 8 **Unit 1's** and 8 **Unit 2's**.
4. Cut 4 **squares** 1¹/2" x 1¹/2" from dark red solid fabric. Cut red print and blue print scraps into 1¹/2"w **strips** for logs. (Depending on location in block, you will need strips varying in length from 5¹/2" to 16".)
5. Using **squares** and **strips**, follow Steps 10 - 13 of **Assembling the Quilt Top**, page 13, to make 4 **Unit 3's**.
6. Follow Steps 15 - 17 of **Assembling the Quilt Top**, page 14, to complete 4 **Blocks**.
7. Referring to **Pillow Top** diagram, sew **Blocks** together to make **Pillow Top**.
8. Follow **Quilting**, page 151, to mark, layer, and quilt using **Quilting Diagram**, page 14, as a suggestion. Our pillow top is hand quilted.
9. Follow **Pillow Finishing**, page 150, to complete pillow with welting.

STARRY WALL HANGING

SKILL LEVEL: 1 2 3 4 5
BLOCK SIZE: 9" x 9"
WALL HANGING SIZE: 25" x 52"

YARDAGE REQUIREMENTS

Yardage is based on 45"w fabric.

■ 1³/4 yds of floral print for border
◩ 3/4 yd *total* of assorted blue prints
◩ 5/8 yd *total* of assorted red prints
⊞ 1/4 yd *each* of tan/red print and tan/blue print
■ 1/8 yd of dark red solid
1⁵/8 yds for backing
3/4 yd for binding
29" x 56" batting

CUTTING OUT THE PIECES

All measurements include a ¹/4" seam allowance. Follow Rotary Cutting, page 144, to cut fabric.

1. **From floral print for border:** ■
   • Cut 2 lengthwise **side borders** 3³/4" x 56".
   • Cut 2 lengthwise **top/bottom borders** 3³/4" x 29".
2. **From assorted blue prints:** ◩
   • Cut 14 **strips** 1¹/2"w.
3. **From assorted red prints:** ◩
   • Cut 12 **strips** 1¹/2"w.
4. **From tan/red print and tan/blue print:** ⊞
   • Cut 3 **strips** 1¹/2"w from *each* fabric.
5. **From dark red solid:** ■
   • Cut 10 **squares** 1¹/2" x 1¹/2".

MAKING THE WALL HANGING

*Follow **Piecing and Pressing**, page 146, to make wall hanging top.*

1. Using tan print **strips**, follow Steps 1 - 3 of **Assembling the Quilt Top**, page 12, to cut 40 **diamond A's** and 40 **diamond B's**.
2. Using red and blue print **strips**, follow Steps 4 - 7 of **Assembling the Quilt Top**, page 12, to cut 20 **red trapezoids** and 20 **blue trapezoids**. (You will need 2 matching **red** and 2 matching **blue trapezoids** for each of 10 **Blocks**.)
3. Follow Steps 8 and 9 of **Assembling the Quilt Top**, page 13, to make 20 **Unit 1's** and 20 **Unit 2's**.
4. Using **squares** and red and blue print **strips**, follow Steps 10 - 13 of **Assembling the Quilt Top**, page 13, to make 10 **Unit 3's**.
5. Follow Steps 15 - 17 of **Assembling the Quilt Top**, page 14, to complete 10 **Blocks**.
6. Referring to **Wall Hanging Top Diagram**, sew **Blocks** together to make center section of wall hanging top.
7. Follow **Adding Mitered Borders**, page 151, to add **borders** to center section to complete **Wall Hanging Top**.
8. Follow **Quilting**, page 151, to mark, layer, and quilt using **Quilting Diagram**, page 14, as a suggestion. Our wall hanging is hand quilted.
9. Cut a 22" square of binding fabric. Follow **Binding**, page 155, to bind wall hanging using 2¹/₂"w bias binding with mitered corners.

Wall Hanging Top Diagram

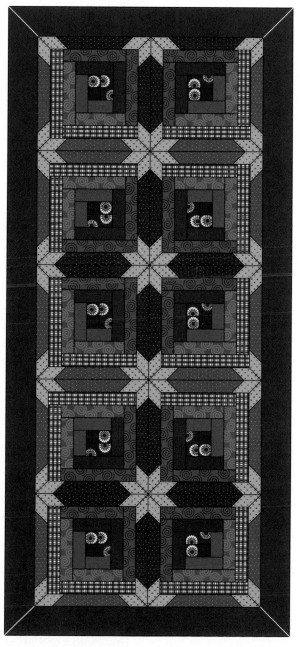

MISSOURI PUZZLE COLLECTION

Many puzzling questions about the vast western wilderness were solved by the great Lewis and Clark expedition through the Missouri River Valley. The explorers charted rich timberlands and discovered a wealth of wild game, sparking the first wave of settlers to flock into the territory. Echoing the rugged paths cleared by those pioneers, the Missouri Puzzle pattern boldly represents their trailblazing spirit. The secret to our quilt is really no puzzle at all — it's created using easy strip sets and grid-pieced triangle-squares! Set together without sashing, the blocks produce an intriguing secondary design of Ohio Stars.

he Ohio Stars that make a surprise appearance in the Missouri Puzzle quilt also shine on our table topper (below). Easy triangle-squares and small white squares are assembled around a large plain square to create the pattern, leaving ample room for a flourish of quilting designs. Accented with a strip-pieced border and Nine-Patch corner squares, the wall hanging (opposite) is made with four of the "puzzle-ing" quilt blocks.

MISSOURI PUZZLE QUILT

SKILL LEVEL: 1 2 3 4 5
BLOCK SIZE: 15" x 15"
QUILT SIZE: 91" x 106"

YARDAGE REQUIREMENTS

Yardage is based on 45"w fabric.

- ■ 5⅝ yds of red solid
- □ 5½ yds of white solid
- ■ 2⅝ yds of navy solid
  8¼ yds for backing
  1⅛ yds for binding
  120" x 120" batting

CUTTING OUT THE PIECES

All measurements include a ¼" seam allowance. Follow
Rotary Cutting, page 144, to cut fabric.

1. **From red solid:** ■
   - Cut 44 **strips** 1½"w.
   - Cut 7 strips 17"w. From these strips, cut
     13 **rectangles** 17" x 21" for triangle-squares.

2. **From white solid:** □
   - Cut 18 strips 3½"w. From these strips, cut
     210 **squares** 3½" x 3½".
   - Cut 7 strips 17"w. From these strips, cut
     13 **rectangles** 17" x 21" for triangle-squares.

3. **From navy solid:** ■
   - Cut 52 **strips** 1½"w.

ASSEMBLING THE QUILT TOP

Follow Piecing and Pressing, page 146, to make quilt top.

1. To make triangle-squares, place 1 white and 1 red
   rectangle right sides together. Referring to **Fig. 1**,
   follow **Making Triangle-Squares**, page 147, to
   make 40 **triangle-squares**. Repeat with remaining
   rectangles to make a total of 520 **triangle-squares**.
   (You will need 504 and have 16 left over.)

Fig. 1

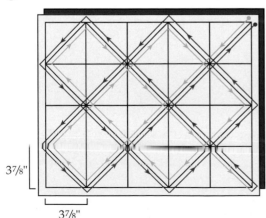

3⅞"
3⅞"

triangle-square (make 520)

2. Sew 3 **strips** together to make **Strip Set A**. Make
   12 **Strip Set A's**. Cut across **Strip Set A's** at 1½"
   intervals to make 336 **Unit 1's**.

Strip Set A (make 12)   **Unit 1 (make 336)**

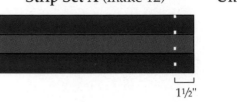

1½"

3. Sew 3 **strips** together to make **Strip Set B**. Make
   20 **Strip Set B's**. Cut across **Strip Set B's** at 1½"
   intervals to make 168 **Unit 2's**. Cut across remaining
   Strip Set B's at 3½" intervals to make 168
   Unit 3's.

Strip Set B (make 20)   **Unit 2 (make 168)**

1½"

Unit 3 (make 168)

3½"

4. Sew 2 **Unit 1's** and 1 **Unit 2** together to make
   Unit 4. Make 168 **Unit 4's**.

Unit 4 (make 168)

5. Sew 4 **triangle-squares** and 1 **square** together to
   make **Unit 5**. Make 84 **Unit 5's**.

Unit 5 (make 84)

6. Sew 2 **triangle-squares**, 2 **Unit 4's**, and 1 **Unit 3** together to make **Unit 6**. Make 84 **Unit 6's**.

Unit 6 (make 84)

7. Sew 3 **squares** and 2 **Unit 3's** together to make **Unit 7**. Make 42 **Unit 7's**.

Unit 7 (make 42)

8. Sew 2 **Unit 5's**, 2 **Unit 6's**, and 1 **Unit 7** together to make **Block**. Make 42 **Blocks**.

Block (make 42)

9. Sew 6 **Blocks** together to make **Row**. Make 7 **Rows**.

10. Referring to **Quilt Top Diagram**, page 24, sew **Rows** together to complete **Quilt Top**.

COMPLETING THE QUILT
1. Follow **Quilting**, page 151, to mark, layer, and quilt using **Quilting Diagram** as a suggestion. Our quilt is hand quilted.
2. Cut a 34" square of binding fabric. Follow **Binding**, page 155, to bind quilt using $2^{1}/_{2}$"w bias binding with mitered corners.

Quilting Diagram

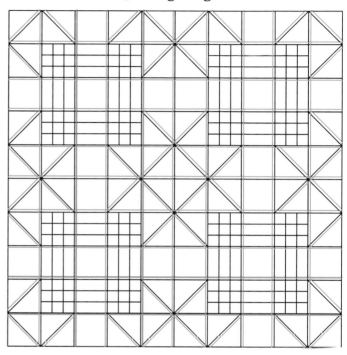

Row (make 7)

MISSOURI PUZZLE WALL HANGING

SKILL LEVEL: 1 2 3 4 5
BLOCK SIZE: 15" x 15"
WALL HANGING SIZE: 37" x 37"

YARDAGE REQUIREMENTS

Yardage is based on 45"w fabric.

■ 1³/₈ yds of red solid
□ 1¹/₈ yds of white solid
■ ⁷/₈ yd of navy solid
  1¹/₄ yds for backing and hanging sleeve
  ³/₄ yd for binding
  40" x 40" batting

CUTTING OUT THE PIECES

All measurements include a ¹/₄" seam allowance. Follow Rotary Cutting, page 144, to cut fabric.

1. **From red solid:** ■
    - Cut 7 **strips** 1¹/₂"w.
    - Cut 4 **border strips** 1¹/₂" x 30¹/₂".
    - Cut 1 **rectangle** 17" x 25" for triangle-squares.

2. **From white solid:** □
    - Cut 2 **strips** 3¹/₂"w. From these strips, cut 20 **squares** 3¹/₂" x 3¹/₂".
    - Cut 1 **rectangle** 17" x 25" for triangle-squares.

3. **From navy solid:** ■
    - Cut 8 **strips** 1¹/₂"w.
    - Cut 8 **border strips** 1¹/₂" x 30¹/₂".

ASSEMBLING THE WALL HANGING TOP

Follow Piecing and Pressing, page 146, to make wall hanging top.

1. To make triangle-squares, place white and red **rectangles** right sides together. Referring to **Fig. 1**, follow **Making Triangle-Squares**, page 147, to make 48 **triangle-squares**.

Fig. 1

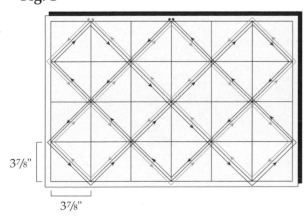

37/8"

37/8"

triangle-square (make 48)

2. Follow Step 2 of **Assembling the Quilt Top**, page 22, to make 40 **Unit 1's** from 2 **Strip Set A's**. Follow Step 3 to make 20 **Unit 2's** and 16 **Unit 3's** from 3 **Strip Set B's**.

Unit 1 (make 40)	**Unit 2** (make 20)	**Unit 3** (make 16)

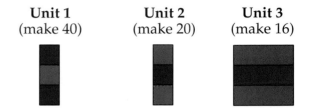

3. Follow Steps 4 - 7 of **Assembling the Quilt Top**, page 22, to make 20 **Unit 4's**, 8 **Unit 5's**, 8 **Unit 6's**, and 4 **Unit 7's**.

Unit 4 (make 20)

Unit 5 (make 8)

Unit 6 (make 8)

Unit 7 (make 4)

4. Sew 2 **Unit 5's**, 2 **Unit 6's**, and 1 **Unit 7** together to make **Block**. Make 4 **Blocks**.

Block (make 4)

5. Referring to **Wall Hanging Top Diagram**, sew **Blocks** together to make center section of wall hanging top.

6. Sew 3 **border strips** together to make **Border Unit**. Make 4 **Border Units**.

Border Unit (make 4)

7. Sew 1 **Border Unit** each to top and bottom of center section. Sew 1 **Unit 4** to each end of remaining **Border Units**. Sew **Border Units** to sides of center section to complete **Wall Hanging Top**.

COMPLETING THE WALL HANGING

1. Follow **Quilting**, page 151, to mark, layer, and quilt using **Quilting Diagram** as a suggestion. Our wall hanging is hand quilted.

2. Cut a 22" square of binding fabric. Follow **Binding**, page 155, to bind quilt using 2¹/₂"w bias binding with mitered corners.

Quilting Diagram

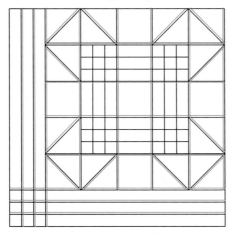

Wall Hanging Top Diagram

TABLE TOPPER

BLOCK SIZE: 15" x 15"
TABLE TOPPER SIZE: 46" x 46"

YARDAGE REQUIREMENTS

Yardage is based on 45"w fabric.

☐ 2 yds of white solid
■ ⁷/₈ yd of red solid
2³/₄ yds for backing
³/₄ yd for binding
49" x 49" batting

CUTTING OUT THE PIECES

*All measurements include a ¹/₄" seam allowance. Follow **Rotary Cutting**, page 144, to cut fabric.*

1. **From white solid:** ☐
   - Cut 3 strips 3¹/₂"w. From these strips, cut 36 **squares** 3¹/₂" x 3¹/₂".
   - Cut 3 strips 9¹/₂"w. From these strips, cut 9 **large squares** 9¹/₂" x 9¹/₂".
   - Cut 1 strip 25"w. From this strip, cut 3 **rectangles** 13" x 25" for triangle-squares.

2. **From red solid:** ■
   - Cut 1 strip 25"w. From this strip, cut 3 **rectangles** 13" x 25" for triangle-squares.

MAKING THE TABLE TOPPER

*Follow **Piecing and Pressing**, page 146, to make table topper.*

1. To make triangle-squares, place 1 white and 1 red **rectangle** right sides together. Referring to **Fig. 1**, follow **Making Triangle-Squares**, page 147, to make 36 **triangle-squares**. Repeat with remaining **rectangles** to make a total of 108 **triangle-squares**.

Fig. 1

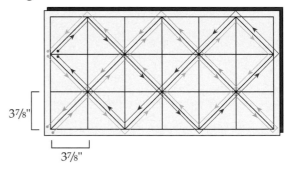

3⁷/₈"

3⁷/₈"

triangle-square (make 108)

2. Sew 2 **triangle-squares** and 1 **square** together to make **Unit 1**. Make 18 **Unit 1's**.

Unit 1 (make 18)

3. Sew 4 **triangle-squares** and 1 **square** together to make **Unit 2**. Make 18 **Unit 2's**.

Unit 2 (make 18)

4. Sew 2 **Unit 1's** and 1 **large square** together to make **Unit 3**. Make 9 **Unit 3's**.

Unit 3 (make 9)

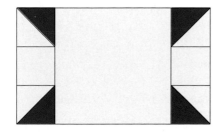

5. Sew 2 **Unit 2's** and 1 **Unit 3** together to make **Block**. Make 9 **Blocks**.

Block (make 9)

6. Sew 3 **Blocks** together to make **Row**. Make 3 **Rows**.

Row (make 3)

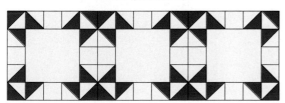

7. Referring to **Table Topper Diagram**, sew **Rows** together to complete **Table Topper Top**.
8. Follow **Quilting**, page 151, to mark, layer, and quilt using **Quilting Diagram** as a suggestion. Our table topper is hand quilted.
9. Cut a 24" square of binding fabric. Follow **Binding**, page 155, to bind table topper using 2^1/$_2$"w bias binding with mitered corners.

Table Topper Diagram

Quilting Diagram

27

PRAIRIE STARS

Just as the big, open skies above America's fruited plains are illuminated with a multitude of brilliant stars, our Prairie Stars quilt shines with the country style of eight-pointed star motifs. The pattern — sometimes known as Blazing Star, Star of the East, or Morning Star — is a scaled-down version of the majestic Lone Star. To simplify each block, we used strip-pieced sets to cut the diamond pieces with accuracy and ease. The result is a dazzling arrangement of 30 blocks set in straight rows with simple sashing. Resembling a tranquil horizon, the wide blue print border is spacious enough for heavenly quilting.

PRAIRIE STARS QUILT

SKILL LEVEL: 1 2 3 4 5
BLOCK SIZE: 12" x 12"
QUILT SIZE: 92" x 106"

YARDAGE REQUIREMENTS
Yardage is based on 45"w fabric.

- 4 yds of red print for sashing and inner borders
- 3½ yds *total* of assorted blue prints
- 3½ yds *total* of assorted red prints
- 3⅜ yds of blue print for outer borders
- 2½ yds of white solid
  8⅜ yds for backing
  1 yd for binding
  120" x 120" batting

CUTTING OUT THE PIECES
All measurements include a ¼" seam allowance. Follow
Rotary Cutting, page 144, to cut fabric.

1. **From red print for sashing and inner borders:**
   - Cut 9 strips 2½"w. From these strips, cut 25 **short sashing strips** 2½" x 12½".
   - Cut 2 lengthwise **side inner borders** 2½" x 109".
   - Cut 2 lengthwise **top/bottom inner borders** 2½" x 95".
   - Cut 4 lengthwise **long sashing strips** 2½" x 82½".

2. **From assorted blue prints:**
   - For *each* of 15 **Block A's,** cut 2 *different* **strips** 1¾"w.
   - For *each* of 15 **Block B's,** cut 2 *matching* **strips** 1¾"w.

3. **From assorted red prints:**
   - For *each* of 15 **Block A's,** cut 2 *matching* **strips** 1¾"w.
   - For *each* of 15 **Block B's,** cut 2 *different* **strips** 1¾"w.

4. **From blue print for outer borders:**
   - Cut 2 lengthwise **side outer borders** 10" x 109".
   - Cut 2 lengthwise **top/bottom outer borders** 10" x 95".

5. **From white solid:**
   - Cut 12 strips 4"w. From these strips, cut 120 **squares** 4" x 4".
   - Cut 5 strips 6¼"w. From these strips, cut 30 squares 6¼" x 6¼". Cut squares twice diagonally to make 120 **triangles.**

ASSEMBLING THE QUILT TOP
Follow Piecing and Pressing, page 116, to make quilt top

1. For Block A, choose 2 *different* blue print **strips** and 2 *matching* red print **strips.** Sew **strips** together, adding each blue print **strip** 1¾" from the end of red print **strip** to make **Strip Sets A** and **B.**

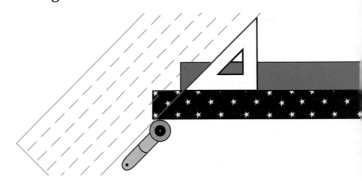

Strip Set A (make 1)

Strip Set B (make 1)

2. Referring to **Fig. 1,** use a large right-angle triangle aligned with seam to determine an accurate 45° cutting line. Use rotary cutter and rotary cutting ruler to trim uneven ends from one end of **Strip Set A** and **Strip Set B.**

Fig. 1

3. Aligning the 45° mark (shown in yellow) on the rotary cutting ruler with seam and aligning the 1¾" mark with cut edge made in Step 2, cut across **Strip Sets** at 1¾" intervals as shown in **Fig. 2** to cut 8 **Unit 1's** from **Strip Set A** and 8 **Unit 2's** from **Strip Set B.**

Fig. 2

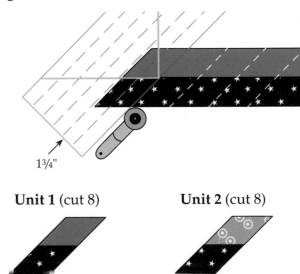

Unit 1 (cut 8)   **Unit 2** (cut 8)

4. When making **Unit 3's**, refer to **Fig. 3** to match long edges of units. Seams will cross 1/4" from cut edges of fabric. Pin and stitch as shown in **Fig. 3**. Sew 1 **Unit 1** and 1 **Unit 2** together to make **Unit 3**. Make 8 **Unit 3's**.

Fig. 3

Unit 3 (make 8)

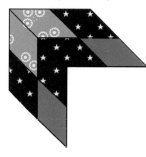

5. To make **Unit 4**, place 2 **Unit 3's** right sides together, carefully matching edges and seams; pin. Stitch in direction shown in **Fig. 4**, ending stitching 1/4" from edge of fabric (you may find it helpful to mark a small dot at this point before sewing) and backstitching at end of seam. Make 4 **Unit 4's**.

Fig. 4   **Unit 4** (make 4)

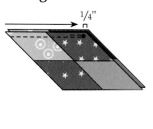

6. Sew **Unit 4's** together to make **Star**, ending stitching 1/4" from outer edges and backstitching at end of each seam.

Star

7. Follow Steps 2 - 4 of **Working with Diamonds and Set-in Seams**, page 148, to sew **triangles**, then **squares** to **Star** to make **Block A**.

Block A

8. Repeat Steps 1 - 7 to make 15 **Block A's**.
9. For Block B, choose 2 *different* red print **strips** and 2 *matching* blue print **strips**. Sew **strips** together, adding each red print **strip** 1³/4" from the end of blue print **strip** to make **Strip Sets C** and **D**.

Strip Set C (make 1)

Strip Set D (make 1)

10. Repeat Steps 2 and 3 to cut 8 **Unit 5's** from **Strip Set C** and 8 **Unit 6's** from **Strip Set D**.

Unit 5 (cut 8)   **Unit 6** (cut 8)

11. Referring to **Block B** diagram, repeat Steps 4 - 7 to make **Block B**.

Block B

12. Repeat Steps 9 - 11 to make 15 **Block B's**.

13. Referring to **Quilt Top Diagram** and alternating **Block A's** and **Block B's**, sew 6 **Blocks** and 5 **short sashing strips** together to make vertical **Row**. Make 5 vertical **Rows**. Sew **Rows** and **long sashing strips** together to make center section of quilt top.

14. Sew **borders** together to make **Border Unit**. Make 2 **Side Border Units** and 2 **Top/Bottom Border Units**.

Border Unit

15. Follow **Adding Mitered Borders**, page 151, to attach **Top/Bottom Border Units** and **Side Border Units** to center section to complete **Quilt Top**.

COMPLETING THE QUILT

1. Follow **Quilting**, page 151, to mark, layer, and quilt using **Quilting Diagram** as a suggestion. Our quilt is hand quilted.

2. Cut a 33" square of binding fabric. Follow **Binding**, page 155, to bind quilt using 2¹/₂"w bias binding with mitered corners.

Quilting Diagram

CAKE STAND COLLECTION

The tantalizing aromas of cinnamon, brown sugar, and cocoa wafting through every room made baking day a special time in Colonial homes. Fresh-from-the-oven delicacies filled the kitchen as the breads and pastries for the week were lovingly prepared. Representing the dessert pedestals on which those sweets were displayed, our Cake Stand quilt is a confection of simple elements. A handy grid technique makes it easy to create the large and small triangle-squares that form the blocks, which are similar to many traditional basket patterns. Plain white squares offset the pieced motifs that are set on point and assembled in diagonal rows. Edged with a series of basic borders, this classic quilt is really a piece of cake!

Dessert time will be extra sweet when the kitchen is accented with our Cake Stand coordinates. Beautiful wreath quilting is the icing on this Cake Stand wall hanging (below). It's fashioned with five pieced blocks that are set on point and finished with contrasting sashing and borders. The checkerboard chair cushions (opposite) are simple to create using rotary cut squares and a purchased cushion form. A delightful backdrop for a coffee break, our table runner completes the collection with homemade goodness.

CAKE STAND QUILT

SKILL LEVEL: 1 2 3 4 5
BLOCK SIZE: 6" x 6"
QUILT SIZE: 76" x 93"

Like many antique quilts, our Cake Stand quilt has irregular borders that are somewhat quirky in their arrangement and colors. With our instructions, you can make a quilt with four mitered borders as shown in the Quilt Top Diagram, page 41.

YARDAGE REQUIREMENTS
Yardage is based on 45"w fabric.

☐ 6 yds of cream solid

■ 3 yds of navy solid

■ 3 yds of red solid
5³/4 yds for backing
1 yd for binding
90" x 108" batting

CUTTING OUT THE PIECES
All measurements include a ¼" seam allowance. Follow **Rotary Cutting**, *page 144, to cut fabric.*

1. **From cream solid:** ☐
   - Cut 8 strips 6¹/2"w. From these strips, cut 48 **setting squares** 6¹/2" x 6¹/2".
   - Cut 2 strips 9³/4"w. From these strips, cut 7 squares 9³/4" x 9³/4". Cut squares twice diagonally to make 28 **side triangles**.
   - Cut 5 strips 1¹/2"w. From these strips, cut 126 **squares** 1¹/2" x 1¹/2".
   - Cut 5 strips 4¹/2"w. From these strips, cut 126 **rectangles** 1¹/2" x 4¹/2".
   - Cut 2 lengthwise **wide side border pieces** 3¹/2" x 96".
   - Cut 2 lengthwise **narrow side border pieces** 2" x 96".
   - Cut 2 lengthwise **wide top/bottom border pieces** 3¹/2" x 79".
   - Cut 2 lengthwise **narrow top/bottom border pieces** 2" x 79".
   - From remaining fabric width, cut 7 **large rectangles** 11" x 19" for small triangle-squares.
   - Cut 2 squares 5¹/8" x 5¹/8". Cut squares once diagonally to make 4 **corner triangles**.

2. **From navy solid:** ■
   - Cut 2 lengthwise **side border pieces** 1¹/2" x 96".
   - Cut 2 lengthwise **top/bottom border pieces** 1¹/2" x 79".
   - From remaining fabric width, cut 7 **large rectangles** 11" x 19" for small triangle-squares.
   - Cut 2 **large squares** 21" x 21" for large triangle-squares.

3. **From red solid:** ■
   - Cut 2 lengthwise **side border pieces** 2¹/2" x 96".
   - Cut 2 lengthwise **top/bottom border pieces** 2¹/2" x 79".

- Cut 2 **large squares** 21" x 21" for large triangle-squares.

ASSEMBLING THE QUILT TOP
Follow **Piecing and Pressing**, *page 146, to make quilt top.*

1. To make small triangle-squares, place 1 cream and 1 navy **large rectangle** right sides together. Referring to **Fig. 1**, follow **Making Triangle-Squares**, page 147, to make 90 **small triangle-squares**. Repeat with remaining **large rectangles** to make a total of 630 **small triangle-squares**.

Fig. 1

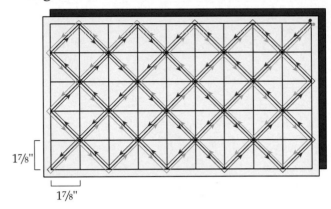

17/8"

17/8"

small triangle-square (make 630)

2. To make large triangle-squares, place 1 red and 1 navy **large square** right sides together. Referring to **Fig. 2**, follow **Making Triangle-Squares**, page 147, to make 32 **large triangle-squares**. Repeat with remaining **large squares** to make a total of 64 **large triangle-squares**. (You will need 63 and have 1 left over.)

Fig. 2

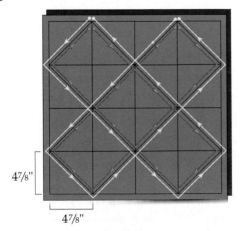

47/8"

47/8"

large triangle-square (make 64)

3. Sew 4 **small triangle-squares** together to make **Unit 1**. Make 63 **Unit 1's**.

Unit 1 (make 63)

4. Sew 4 **small triangle-squares** and 1 **square** together to make **Unit 2**. Make 63 **Unit 2's**.

Unit 2 (make 63)

5. Sew 1 **Unit 1** and 1 **large triangle-square** together to make **Unit 3**. Make 63 **Unit 3's**.

Unit 3 (make 63)

6. Sew 1 **Unit 3** and 1 **Unit 2** together to make **Unit 4**. Make 63 **Unit 4's**.

Unit 4 (make 63)

7. Sew 1 **small triangle-square** and 1 **rectangle** together to make **Unit 5**. Make 63 **Unit 5's**.

Unit 5 (make 63)

8. Sew 1 **square**, 1 **small triangle-square**, and 1 **rectangle** together to make **Unit 6**. Make 63 **Unit 6's**.

Unit 6 (make 63)

9. Sew 1 **Unit 4**, 1 **Unit 5**, and 1 **Unit 6** together to make **Block**. Make 63 **Blocks**.

Block (make 63)

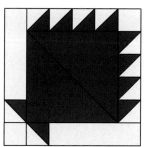

10. Referring to **Assembly Diagram**, page 40, sew **corner triangles**, **side triangles**, **Blocks**, and **setting squares** into diagonal rows; sew rows together to make center section of quilt top.

11. Sew 1 navy, 1 narrow cream, 1 red, and 1 wide cream **top/bottom border pieces** together to make **Top/Bottom Border Unit**. Make 2 **Top/Bottom Border Units**. Using **side border pieces**, repeat to make **Side Border Unit**. Make 2 **Side Border Units**.

Border Unit

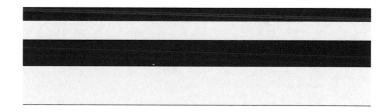

12. Referring to **Quilt Top Diagram**, page 41, follow **Adding Mitered Borders**, page 151, to sew **Border Units** to center section to complete **Quilt Top**.

COMPLETING THE QUILT

1. Follow **Quilting**, page 151, to mark, layer, and quilt using **Quilting Diagram**, page 41, as a suggestion. Our quilt is hand quilted.
2. Cut a 32" square of binding fabric. Follow **Binding**, page 155, to bind quilt using 2¹/₂"w bias binding with mitered corners.

Quilt Top Diagram

Quilting Diagram

CAKE STAND WALL HANGING

SKILL LEVEL: 1 2 3 4 5
BLOCK SIZE: 6" x 6"
WALL HANGING SIZE: 26" x 26"

YARDAGE REQUIREMENTS
Yardage is based on 45"w fabric.

■ ⅝ yd of red print
□ ½ yd of cream print
■ ½ yd of navy print
    ⅞ yd for backing and hanging sleeve
    ⅝ yd for binding
    28" x 28" batting

CUTTING OUT THE PIECES
All measurements include a ¼" seam allowance. Follow
***Rotary Cutting**, page 144, to cut fabric.*

1. **From red print:** ■
   - Cut 1 strip 6½"w. From this strip, cut 16 **sashing strips** 1½" x 6½".
   - Cut 4 **borders** 3" x 20⅜".
   - Cut 1 **large rectangle** 6" x 16" for large triangle-squares.

2. **From cream print:** □
   - Cut 2 strips 1½"w. From these strips, cut 10 **rectangles** 1½" x 4½" and 10 **squares** 1½" x 1½".
   - Cut 1 **large square** 11" x 11" for small triangle-squares.
   - Cut 1 square 9¾" x 9¾". Cut square twice diagonally to make 4 **side triangles**.
   - Cut 2 squares 5⅛" x 5⅛". Cut squares once diagonally to make 4 **corner triangles**.

3. **From navy print:** ■
   - Cut 1 **large square** 11" x 11" for small triangle-squares.
   - Cut 1 **large rectangle** 6" x 16" for large triangle-squares.
   - Cut 4 **corner squares** 3" x 3".
   - Cut 12 **sashing squares** 1½" x 1½".

ASSEMBLING THE WALL HANGING TOP
*Follow **Piecing and Pressing**, page 146, to make wall hanging top.*

1. To make small triangle-squares, place cream and navy **large squares** right sides together. Referring to **Fig. 1**, follow **Making Triangle-Squares**, page 147, to make 50 **small triangle-squares**.

   Fig. 1

   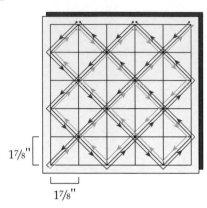

   17⅞"
   17⅞"

   small triangle-square (make 50)

2. To make large triangle-squares, place navy and red **large rectangles** right sides together. Referring to **Fig. 2**, follow **Making Triangle-Squares**, page 147, to make 6 **large triangle-squares**. (You will need 5 and have 1 left over.)

   Fig. 2

   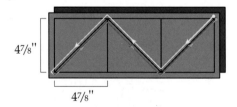

   4⅞"
   4⅞"

   large triangle-square (make 6)

3. Follow Steps 3 - 9 of **Assembling the Quilt Top**, page 39, to make 5 **Blocks**. (You will need 5 **Unit 1's**, 5 **Unit 2's**, 5 **Unit 3's**, 5 **Unit 4's**, 5 **Unit 5's**, and 5 **Unit 6's**.)

4. Referring to **Assembly Diagram**, sew **corner triangles**, **sashing squares**, **sashing strips**, **side triangles**, and **Blocks** together into diagonal **Rows**; sew **Rows** together.

5. Referring to **Fig. 3**, trim **sashing squares** even with raw edges of **side** and **corner triangles** to make center section of wall hanging.

Fig. 3

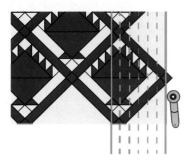

6. Sew 1 **border** each to top and bottom edges of center section. Sew 1 **corner square** to each end of each remaining **border**; sew borders to side edges of center section to complete **Wall Hanging Top**.

COMPLETING THE WALL HANGING

1. Follow **Quilting**, page 151, to mark, layer, and quilt using **Quilting Diagram** as a suggestion. Our wall hanging is hand quilted.
2. Follow **Making a Hanging Sleeve**, page 157, to attach hanging sleeve to wall hanging.
3. Cut an 18" square of binding fabric. Follow **Binding**, page 155, to bind wall hanging using 2¹/₂"w bias binding with mitered corners.

Assembly Diagram

Wall Hanging Top Diagram

Quilting Diagram

CAKE STAND TABLE RUNNER

BLOCK SIZE: 6" x 6"
TABLE RUNNER SIZE: 16" x 65"

YARDAGE REQUIREMENTS
Yardage is based on 45"w fabric.

- ⬛ 1⁷/₈ yds of red print
- ⬜ ³/₄ yd of cream print
- ⬛ ¹/₂ yd of navy print
- 1 yd for backing
- ³/₄ yd for binding
- 20" x 69" batting

CUTTING OUT THE PIECES
All measurements include a ¹/₄" seam allowance. Follow Rotary Cutting, page 144, to cut fabric.

1. **From red print:** ⬛
   - Cut 2 lengthwise **long borders** 3" x 59⁷/₈".
   - From remaining fabric width, cut 1 strip 6¹/₂"w. From this strip, cut 24 **sashing strips** 1¹/₂" x 6¹/₂".
   - Cut 2 **short borders** 3" x 10³/₈".
   - Cut 1 **large rectangle** 6" x 11" for large triangle-squares.

2. **From cream print:** ⬜
   - Cut 2 strips 1¹/₂"w. From these strips, cut 8 **rectangles** 1¹/₂" x 4¹/₂" and 8 **squares** 1¹/₂" x 1¹/₂".
   - Cut 1 **large square** 11" x 11" for small triangle-squares.
   - Cut 3 squares 9³/₄" x 9³/₄". Cut squares twice diagonally to make 12 **side triangles**. (You will need 10 and have 2 left over.)
   - Cut 2 **setting squares** 6¹/₂" x 6¹/₂".
   - Cut 2 squares 5¹/₈" x 5¹/₈". Cut squares once diagonally to make 4 **corner triangles**.

3. **From navy print:** ⬛
   - Cut 1 strip 1¹/₂"w. From this strip, cut 19 **sashing squares** 1¹/₂" x 1¹/₂".
   - Cut 1 **large square** 11" x 11" for small triangle-squares.
   - Cut 1 **large rectangle** 6" x 11" for large triangle-squares.
   - Cut 4 **corner squares** 3" x 3".

ASSEMBLING THE TABLE RUNNER TOP
Follow Piecing and Pressing, page 146, to make table runner top.

1. To make small triangle-squares, follow Step 1 of **Assembling the Wall Hanging Top**, page 42, to make 50 **small triangle-squares**. (You will need 40 and have 10 left over.)

2. To make large triangle-squares, place red and navy **large rectangles** right sides together. Referring to **Fig. 1**, follow **Making Triangle-Squares**, page 147, to make 4 **large triangle-squares**.

Fig. 1

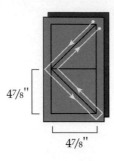

4⁷/₈"

4⁷/₈"

large triangle-square (make 4)

3. Follow Steps 3 - 9 of **Assembling the Quilt Top**, page 39, to make 4 **Blocks**. (You will need 4 **Unit 1's**, 4 **Unit 2's**, 4 **Unit 3's**, 4 **Unit 4's**, 4 **Unit 5's**, and 4 **Unit 6's**.)

4. Referring to **Assembly Diagram**, sew **corner triangles**, **sashing squares**, **sashing strips**, **side triangles**, and **Blocks** together into diagonal rows; sew rows together.

5. Referring to **Fig. 3**, page 43, trim **sashing squares** even with edges of **triangles** to make center section of table runner.

6. Sew 1 **long border** to each long edge of center section. Sew 1 **corner square** to each end of each **short border**; sew borders to short edges of center section to complete **Table Runner Top**.

COMPLETING THE TABLE RUNNER

1. Follow **Quilting**, page 151, to mark, layer, and quilt using **Quilting Diagram** as a suggestion. Our table runner is hand quilted.

2. Cut a 23" square of binding fabric. Follow **Binding**, page 155, to bind table runner using 2¹/₂"w bias binding with mitered corners.

Quilting Diagram

Assembly Diagram

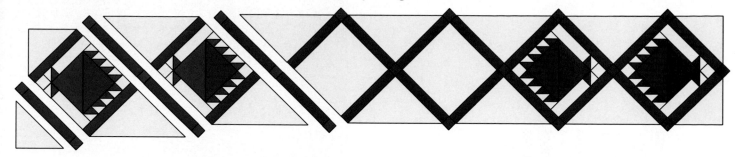

Table Runner Top Diagram

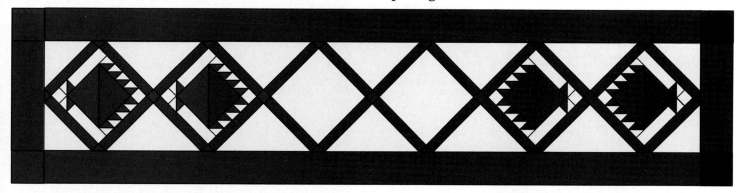

CHECKERBOARD CHAIR CUSHION

Instructions are for 1 chair cushion.

SUPPLIES

purchased 1" thick foam chair cushion form
cream print fabric
red print fabric
fabric for cushion bottom
3"w bias strip for welting
$1/4$" cord for welting
paper for pattern

MAKING THE CHAIR CUSHION

1. To make pattern, place chair cushion form on paper; use a pencil to draw around form. Draw a second line $1/2$" outside drawn line; cut out along outer line.

2. To make chair cushion top, follow **Rotary Cutting**, page 144, to cut $3^1/2$" squares from cream and red print fabrics. Arranging squares in a checkerboard design, follow **Piecing and Pressing**, page 146, to piece a square or rectangle large enough to cover pattern (**Fig. 1**).

Fig. 1

3. Place pattern on wrong side of pieced square or rectangle; use pencil to mark around pattern. Cut out shape along drawn line to make chair cushion top.

4. Use pattern to cut a second shape from fabric for cushion bottom.

5. Follow **Adding Welting to Pillow Top** and **Making the Pillow**, page 158, to make chair cushion with welting.

6. To make **ties**, cut 2 pieces of cream print fabric $2^1/2$" x 32". Fold each piece in half lengthwise with right sides together. Using a $1/4$" seam allowance, sew raw edges together, leaving an opening for turning. Cut corners diagonally and turn right side out; press. Blindstitch openings closed.

7. Matching ends, fold each tie in half. Pin ties in desired positions for chair. Hand stitch ties in place to complete **Chair Cushion**.

DOUBLE NINE-PATCH

A Western-style barbecue wouldn't be complete without a comfy quilt to serve as a picnic spread. With its casual charm, this Double Nine-Patch quilt will please any cowpoke! Look closely at the country chain pattern and you'll see that it's created using doubly easy elements: small strip-pieced Nine-Patch units are set together to form large Nine-Patch blocks! The blocks are then set on point and alternated with plain setting squares to form the chain design. Completed with basic borders, this quilt is so simple to create that seldom is heard a discouraging word — even from beginners!

DOUBLE NINE-PATCH QUILT

SKILL LEVEL: 1 2 3 4 5
BLOCK SIZE: 11¼" x 11¼"
QUILT SIZE: 76" x 76"

Although the maker of our antique quilt dealt with many bias edges in order to match the direction of the checks in her quilt top, our instructions eliminate these bias edges and substitute a small red print for the checked fabric.

YARDAGE REQUIREMENTS
Yardage is based on 45"w fabric.

■ 4¾ yds of red print
 4 yds of navy print
4¾ yds for backing
1 yd for binding
90" x 108" batting

CUTTING OUT THE PIECES
All measurements include a ¼" seam allowance. Follow Rotary Cutting, page 144, to cut fabric.

1. **From red print:**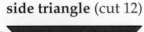
   - Cut 15 **strips** 1¾"w.
   - Cut 8 strips 4¼"w. From these strips, cut 64 **squares** 4¼" x 4¼".
   - Cut 4 lengthwise **outer borders** 3½" x 80".
   - From remaining fabric width, cut 9 **setting squares** 11¾" x 11¾".
   - From remaining fabric width, cut 3 squares 17¼" x 17¼". Cut squares twice diagonally to make 12 **side triangles**.

square (cut 3)   **side triangle** (cut 12)

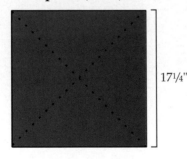

17¼"

   - Cut 2 squares 8⅞" x 8⅞". Cut squares once diagonally to make 4 **corner triangles**.

square (cut 2)   **corner triangle** (cut 4)

8⅞"

2. **From navy print:**
   - Cut 18 **strips** 1¾"w.
   - Cut 4 lengthwise **inner borders** 3" x 80".

ASSEMBLING THE QUILT TOP
Follow Piecing and Pressing, page 146, to make quilt top.

1. Sew 3 **strips** together to make **Strip Set A**. Make 7 **Strip Set A's**. Cut across **Strip Set A's** at 1¾" intervals to make 160 **Unit 1's**.

Strip Set A (make 7)   **Unit 1** (make 160)

1¾"

2. Sew 3 **strips** together to make **Strip Set B**. Make 4 **Strip Set B's**. Cut across **Strip Set B's** at 1¾" intervals to make 80 **Unit 2's**.

Strip Set B (make 4)   **Unit 2** (make 80)

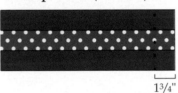

1¾"

3. Sew 2 **Unit 1's** and 1 **Unit 2** together to make **Unit 3**. Make 80 **Unit 3's**.

Unit 3 (make 80)

4. Sew 2 **Unit 3's** and 1 **square** together to make **Unit 4**. Make 32 **Unit 4's**.

Unit 4 (make 32)

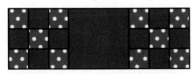

5. Sew 2 **squares** and 1 **Unit 3** together to make **Unit 5**. Make 16 **Unit 5's**.

Unit 5 (make 16)

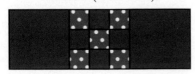

6. Sew 2 **Unit 4's** and 1 **Unit 5** together to make **Block**. Make 16 **Blocks**.

Block (make 16)

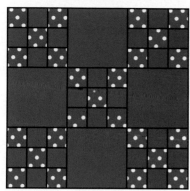

7. Referring to **Assembly Diagram**, page 50, sew **corner triangles**, **side triangles**, **Blocks**, and **setting squares** together into diagonal rows. Sew rows together to make center section of quilt top.

8. Sew 1 **inner border** and 1 **outer border** together to make **Border Unit**. Make 4 **Border Units**.

Border Unit (make 4)

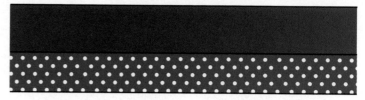

9. Referring to **Quilt Top Diagram**, page 51, follow **Adding Mitered Borders**, page 151, to sew **Border Units** to center section to complete **Quilt Top**.

COMPLETING THE QUILT

1. Follow **Quilting**, page 151, to mark, layer, and quilt using **Quilting Diagram** as a suggestion. Our quilt is hand quilted.
2. Cut a 30" square of binding fabric. Follow **Binding**, page 155, to bind quilt using 2½"w bias binding with mitered corners.

Quilting Diagram

Quilt Top Diagram

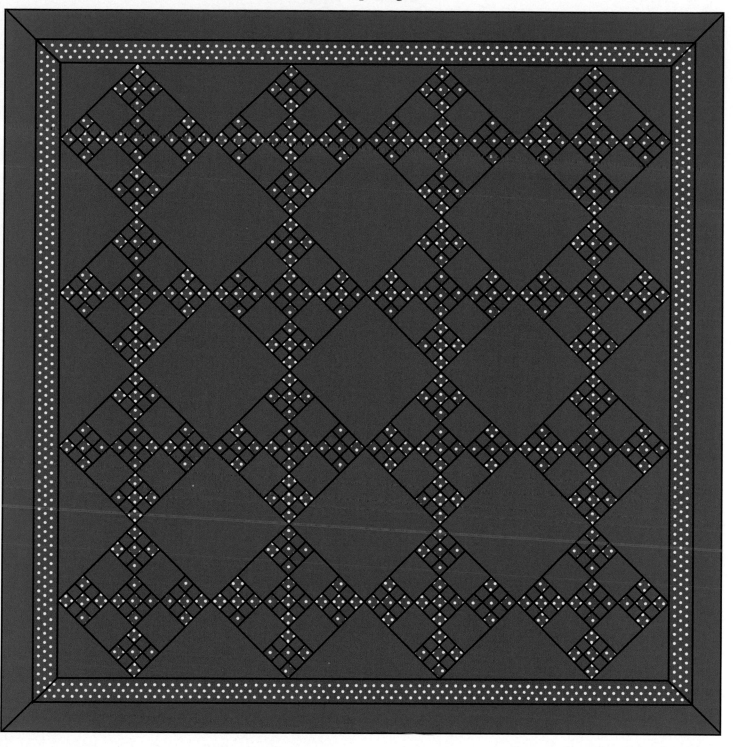

STARS & STRIPES COLLECTION

A *glorious assortment of star-spangled designs makes this quilt a patriotic pleaser! All-American star prints complement the four pieced patterns that create the quilt top. Each block is made with two basic elements: grid-pieced triangle-squares for the stars and quick strip sets for the stripes. For extra accuracy, we used a large square ruler that makes it easy to trim strip sets on the diagonal using a rotary cutter. Simple sashing and two wide borders provide ample room for stellar quilting! The blocks are also a good size for creating matching throw pillows. Just add basic borders and finish the cushions with welted edging.*

Create a galaxy of coordinating throw pillows from our star-struck quilt blocks. Perfect accessories for the quilt, they also make radiant accents for furnishings throughout your home!

54

STARS & STRIPES QUILT

SKILL LEVEL: 1 2 3 4 5
BLOCK SIZE: 14" x 14"
QUILT SIZE: 93" x 109"

YARDAGE REQUIREMENTS
Yardage is based on 45"w fabric.

★ 5⅝ yds of blue print
★ 5⅜ yds of red print
★ 5⅜ yds of cream/red print
☐ 1⅞ yds of cream solid
★ 1¾ yds of cream/blue print
    8½ yds for backing
    1 yd for binding
    120" x 120" batting

You will also need:
    12½" square rotary cutting ruler

CUTTING OUT THE PIECES
All measurements include a ¼" seam allowance. Follow **Rotary Cutting***, page 144, to cut fabric.*

1. **From blue print:** ★
    - Cut 10 strips 1½"w. From these strips, cut 280 **small squares** 1½" x 1½".
    - Cut 5 strips 1¼"w. From these strips, cut 10 **medium rectangles** 1¼" x 15½".
    - Cut 2 strips 2"w. From these strips, cut 10 **small rectangles** 2" x 4½".
    - Cut 1 strip 3¾"w. From this strip, cut 5 squares 3¾" x 3¾". Cut squares once diagonally to make 10 **medium triangles**.
    - Cut 1 strip 6⅞"w. From this strip, cut 5 squares 6⅞" x 6⅞". Cut squares twice diagonally to make 20 **large triangles**.
    - Cut 2 lengthwise **side outer borders** 8½" x 112".
    - Cut 2 lengthwise **top/bottom outer borders** 8½" x 96".
    - Cut 5 squares 2¼" x 2¼". Cut squares once diagonally to make 10 **small triangles**.
    - Cut 4 **rectangles** 15" x 20" for triangle-squares.

2. **From red print:** ★
    - Cut 42 **strips** 1½"w.
    - Cut 2 lengthwise **side middle borders** 5½" x 112".
    - Cut 2 lengthwise **top/bottom middle borders** 5½" x 96".

3. **From cream/red print:** ★
    - Cut 42 **strips** 1½"w.
    - Cut 2 lengthwise **side inner borders** 2½" x 112".
    - Cut 2 lengthwise **top/bottom inner borders** 2½" x 96".
    - Cut 3 lengthwise **long sashing strips** 2½" x 78½".
    - From remaining fabric width, cut 16 **short sashing strips** 2½" x 14½".

4. **From cream solid:** ☐
    - Cut 14 strips 1½"w. From these strips, cut 40 **top/bottom block borders** 1½" x 12½".
    - Cut 20 strips 1½"w. From these strips, cut 40 **side block borders** 1½" x 14½".

5. **From cream/blue print:** ★
    - Cut 5 strips 2½"w. From these strips, cut 70 **medium squares** 2½" x 2½".
    - Cut 4 **rectangles** 15" x 20" for triangle-squares.

MAKING THE BLOCKS
Follow **Piecing and Pressing***, page 146, to make blocks.*
MAKING STAR UNIT
1. To make triangle-squares, place 1 blue and 1 cream/blue **rectangle** right sides together. Referring to **Fig. 1**, follow **Making Triangle-Squares**, page 147, to make 140 **triangle-squares**. Repeat with remaining blue and cream/blue **rectangles** to make a total of 560 **triangle-squares**.

Fig. 1

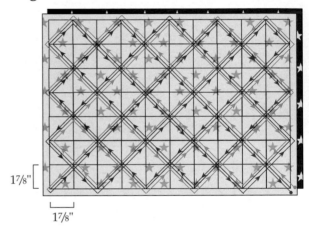

triangle-square (make 560)

2. Sew 2 **triangle-squares** together to make **Unit 1**. Make 280 **Unit 1's**.

Unit 1 (make 280)

3. Sew 2 **small squares** and 1 **Unit 1** together to make **Unit 2**. Make 140 **Unit 2's**.

Unit 2 (make 140)

4. Sew 2 **Unit 1's** and 1 **medium square** together to make **Unit 3**. Make 70 **Unit 3's**.

Unit 3 (make 70)

5. Sew 2 **Unit 2's** and 1 **Unit 3** together to make **Star Unit**. Make 70 **Star Units**.

Star Unit (make 70)

MAKING BLOCK A

1. Sew **strips** together to make **Strip Set A**. Make 5 **Strip Set A's**.

Strip Set A (make 5)

2. Referring to **Fig. 2a**, center square ruler on 1 end of **Strip Set A** with diagonal line on ruler aligned with seamline in center of strip set. Trim fabric extending to the right of ruler. Referring to **Fig. 2b**, turn cut strip set 180° and align previously cut edge with 4½" markings on ruler. Trim fabric extending to the right of ruler to make **Unit 4**. Repeat to make 25 **Unit 4's**.

Fig. 2a

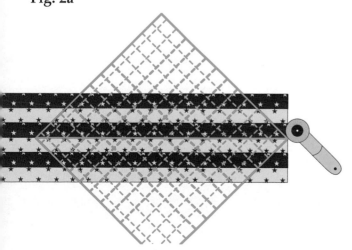

Fig. 2b

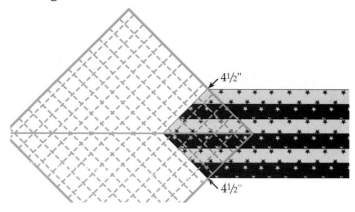

Unit 4 (make 25)

3. Sew 2 **Unit 4's** and 1 **Star Unit** together to make **Unit 5**. Make 10 **Unit 5's**. Sew 2 **Star Units** and 1 **Unit 4** together to make **Unit 6**. Make 5 **Unit 6's**.

Unit 5 (make 10)

Unit 6 (make 5)

4. Sew 2 **Unit 5's** and 1 **Unit 6** together to make **Block A**. Make 5 **Block A's**.

Block A (make 5)

MAKING BLOCK B

1. Sew **strips** together to make **Strip Set B**. Make 3 **Strip Set B's**. Cut across **Strip Set B's** at 4½" intervals to make 20 **Unit 7's**.

Strip Set B (make 3)   **Unit 7** (make 20)

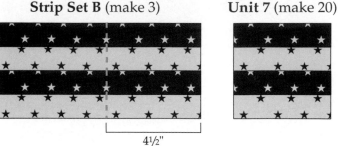

4½"

2. Sew 2 **Star Units** and 1 **Unit 7** together to make **Unit 8**. Make 10 **Unit 8's**. Sew 2 **Unit 7's** and 1 **Star Unit** together to make **Unit 9**. Make 5 **Unit 9's**.

Unit 8 (make 10)

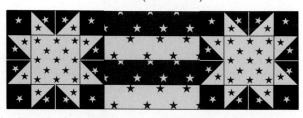

Unit 9 (make 5)

3. Sew 2 **Unit 8's** and 1 **Unit 9** together to make **Block B**. Make 5 **Block B's**.

Block B (make 5)

MAKING BLOCK C

1. Sew **strips** together to make **Strip Set C**. Make 2 **Strip Set C's**.

Strip Set C (make 2)

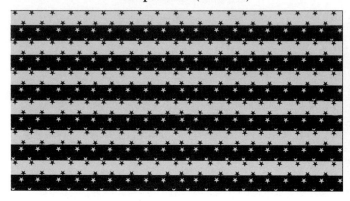

2. Referring to **Fig. 3a**, center square ruler on 1 end of **Strip Set C** with diagonal line on ruler aligned with seamline in center of strip set. Trim fabric extending to the right of ruler. Referring to **Fig. 3b**, turn cut strip set 180° and align previously cut edge with 9" markings on ruler. Trim fabric extending to the right of ruler to cut square 9" x 9". Repeat to cut 5 squares 9" x 9".

Fig. 3a

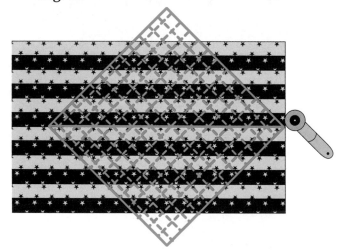

Fig. 3b

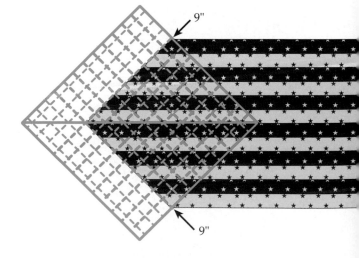

9"

9"

3. Referring to **Fig. 4**, cut squares once diagonally to make 10 **Unit 10's**.

Fig. 4   **Unit 10** (make 10)

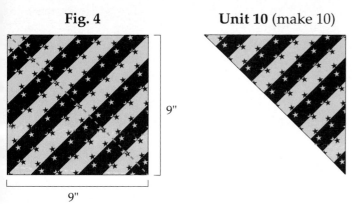

9"

9"

4. Sew 3 **Star Units**, 2 **small rectangles**, 2 **small triangles**, and 2 **medium rectangles** together to make **Unit 11**. Make 5 **Unit 11's**.

Unit 11 (make 5)

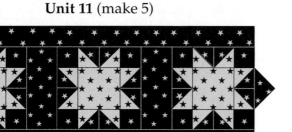

5. Matching centers, sew 2 **Unit 10's** and 1 **Unit 11** together. Trim **Unit 11** even with adjacent edges of **Unit 10's** to make **Block C**. Make 5 **Block C's**.

Block C (make 5)

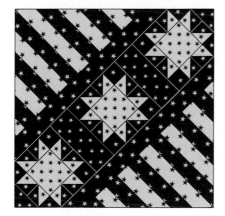

MAKING BLOCK D

1. Sew **strips** together to make 1 **Strip Set D**. Cut across **Strip Set D** at 5¹/₂" intervals to make 5 **Unit 12's**.

Strip Set D (make 1)   **Unit 12** (make 5)

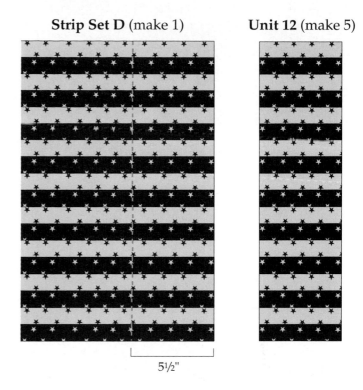

5¹/₂"

2. Sew 2 **large triangles**, 1 **Star Unit**, and 1 **medium triangle** together to make **Unit 13**. Make 10 **Unit 13's**.

Unit 13 (make 10)

3. Matching centers, sew 2 **Unit 13's** and 1 **Unit 12** together. Trim **Unit 12** even with edges of **Unit 13's** to make **Block D**. Make 5 **Block D's**.

Block D (make 5)

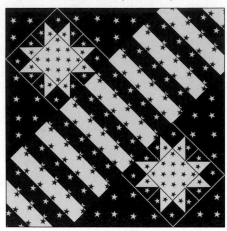

ASSEMBLING THE QUILT TOP

*Follow **Piecing and Pressing**, page 146, to make quilt top.*

1. Sew 1 **top**, 1 **bottom**, and 2 **side block borders** to each **Block**.
2. Referring to **Quilt Top Diagram**, sew 5 **Blocks** and 4 **short sashing strips** together to make vertical **Row**. Make 4 vertical rows.
3. Sew rows and **long sashing strips** together to make center section of quilt top.
4. Referring to **Quilt Top Diagram**, sew 1 each of **side inner**, **middle**, and **outer borders** together to make **Side Border Unit**. Make 2 **Side Border Units**. Repeat with remaining **borders** to make 2 **Top/Bottom Border Units**.
5. Referring to **Quilt Top Diagram**, follow **Adding Mitered Borders**, page 151, to attach **Border Units** to center section to complete **Quilt Top**.

COMPLETING THE QUILT TOP

1. Follow **Quilting**, page 151, to mark, layer, and quilt using **Quilting Diagram** as a suggestion. Our quilt is hand quilted.
2. Cut a 33" square of binding fabric. Follow **Binding**, page 155, to bind quilt using 2$\frac{1}{2}$"w bias binding with mitered corners.

Quilting Diagram

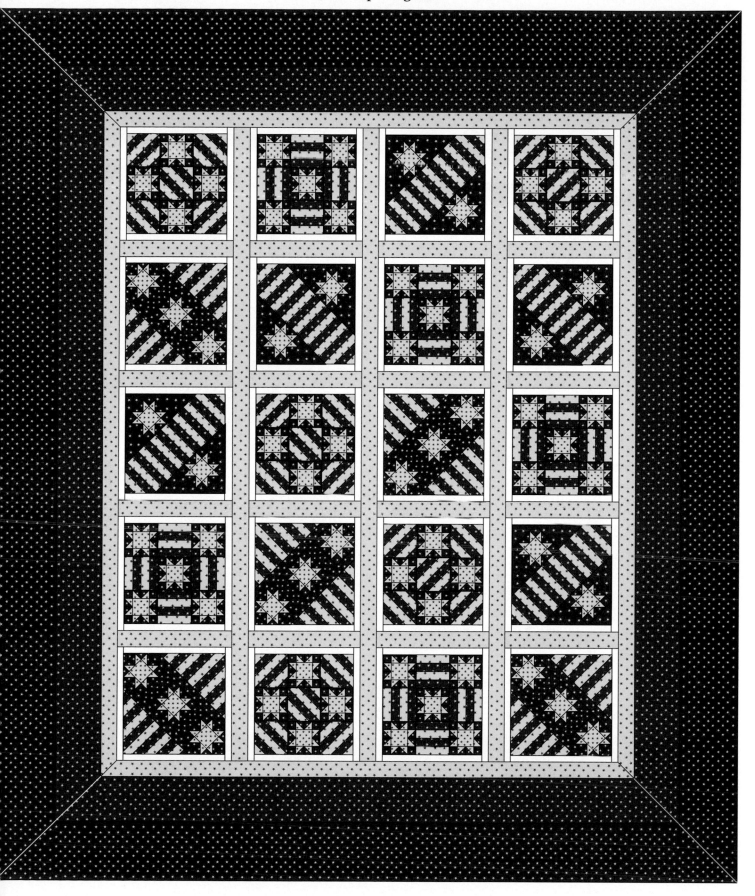

PARADE OF PILLOWS

PILLOW SIZE: 16" x 16"

Our coordinating pillows feature 1 each of Blocks A, B, C, and D from the Stars & Stripes Quilt, page 56.

YARDAGE REQUIREMENTS

Yardage is based on 45"w fabric.

For *each* pillow you will need:
- ⭐ ¼ yd *each* of blue print, cream/blue print, red print, and cream/red print
- ¼ yd for borders
- 2 yds of 2¼"w bias strip for welting
- 20" x 20" piece for pillow top backing
- 16½" x 16½" piece for pillow back
- 2 yds of 7/32" cord for welting
- 20" x 20" batting

You will also need:
- polyester fiberfill

MAKING THE PILLOW TOPS

All measurements include a ¼" seam allowance. Follow Rotary Cutting, page 144, to cut fabric. Follow Piecing and Pressing, page 146, to make pillow tops.

MAKING PILLOW TOP A

1. Cut the following pieces from indicated fabrics:
   From blue print: ⭐
   - Cut 4 **large squares** 6" x 6" for triangle-squares.
   - Cut 16 **small squares** 1½" x 1½".
   From cream/blue print: ⭐
   - Cut 4 **large squares** 6" x 6" for triangle-squares.
   - Cut 4 **squares** 2½" x 2½".
   From red print: ⭐
   - Cut 3 **strips** 1½"w.
   From cream/red print: ⭐
   - Cut 3 **strips** 1½"w.
2. To make triangle-squares, place 1 blue and 1 cream/blue **large square** right sides together. Referring to **Fig. 1**, follow **Making Triangle-Squares**, page 147, to make 8 **triangle-squares**. Repeat with remaining **large squares** to make a total of 32 **triangle-squares**.

Fig. 1

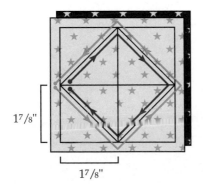

17/8"

17/8"

triangle-square (make 32)

3. Follow Steps 2 - 5 of **Making Star Unit**, page 56, to make 4 **Star Units**. (You will need 16 **Unit 1's**, 8 **Unit 2's**, and 4 **Unit 3's**.)
4. Follow **Making Block A**, page 57, to make 1 block for **Pillow Top A**. (You will need 1 **Strip Set A**, 5 **Unit 4's**, 2 **Unit 5's**, and 1 **Unit 6**.)

Pillow Top A

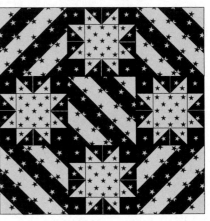

MAKING PILLOW TOP B

1. Cut the following pieces from indicated fabrics:
   From blue print: ⭐
   - Cut 5 **large squares** 6" x 6" for triangle-squares.
   - Cut 20 **small squares** 1½" x 1½".
   From cream/blue print: ⭐
   - Cut 5 **large squares** 6" x 6" for triangle-squares.
   - Cut 5 **squares** 2½" x 2½".
   From red print: ⭐
   - Cut 2 **strips** 1½"w.
   From cream/red print: ⭐
   - Cut 2 **strips** 1½"w.
2. Follow Step 2 of **Making Pillow Top A** to make a total of 40 **triangle-squares**.
3. Follow Steps 2 - 5 of **Making Star Unit**, page 56, to make 5 **Star Units**. (You will need 20 **Unit 1's**, 10 **Unit 2's**, and 5 **Unit 3's**.)
4. Follow **Making Block B**, page 58, to make 1 block for **Pillow Top B**. (You will need 1 **Strip Set B**, 4 **Unit 7's**, 2 **Unit 8's**, and 1 **Unit 9**.)

Pillow Top B

MAKING PILLOW TOP C

1. Cut the following pieces from indicated fabrics:
   From blue print: ★
   - Cut 3 **large squares** 6" x 6" for triangle-squares.
   - Cut 12 **small squares** 1¹/₂" x 1¹/₂".
   - Cut 2 **small rectangles** 2" x 4¹/₂".
   - Cut 2 **medium rectangles** 1¹/₄" x 15¹/₂".
   - Cut 1 square 2¹/₄" x 2¹/₄". Cut square once diagonally to make 2 **small triangles**.
   From cream/blue print: ★
   - Cut 3 **large squares** 6" x 6" for triangle-squares.
   - Cut 3 **squares** 2¹/₂" x 2¹/₂".
   From red print: ★
   - Cut 6 **strips** 1¹/₂" x 13".
   From cream/red print: ★
   - Cut 6 **strips** 1¹/₂" x 13".
2. Follow Step 2 of **Making Pillow Top A** to make a total of 24 **triangle-squares**.
3. Follow Steps 2 - 5 of **Making Star Unit**, page 56, to make 3 **Star Units**. (You will need 12 **Unit 1's**, 6 **Unit 2's**, and 3 **Unit 3's**.)
4. Follow **Making Block C**, page 58, to make 1 block for **Pillow Top C**. (You will need 1 **Strip Set C**, 2 **Unit 10's**, and 1 **Unit 11**.)

Pillow Top C

MAKING PILLOW TOP D

1. Cut the following pieces from indicated fabrics:
   From blue print: ★
   - Cut 1 square 6⁷/₈" x 6⁷/₈". Cut square twice diagonally to make 4 **large triangles**.
   - Cut 1 square 3³/₄" x 3³/₄". Cut square once diagonally to make 2 **medium triangles**.
   - Cut 2 **large squares** 6" x 6" for triangle-squares.
   - Cut 8 **small squares** 1¹/₂" x 1¹/₂".
   From cream/blue print: ★
   - Cut 2 **large squares** 6" x 6" for triangle-squares.
   - Cut 2 **squares** 2¹/₂" x 2¹/₂".
   From red print: ★
   - Cut 9 **strips** 1¹/₂" x 7".
   From cream/red print: ★
   - Cut 9 **strips** 1¹/₂" x 7".
2. Follow Step 2 of **Making Pillow Top A** to make a total of 16 **triangle-squares**.
3. Follow Steps 2 - 5 of **Making Star Unit**, page 56, to make 4 **Star Units**. (You will need 8 **Unit 1's**, 4 **Unit 2's**, and 2 **Unit 3's**.)
4. Follow **Making Block D**, page 59, to make 1 block for **Pillow Top D**. (You will need 1 **Strip Set D**, 1 **Unit 12**, and 2 **Unit 13's**.)

Pillow Top D

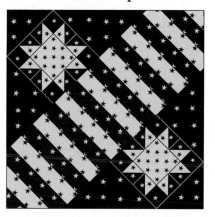

COMPLETING THE PILLOWS

1. For each pillow, cut 4 **borders** 2¹/₂" x 18" from border fabric. Follow **Adding Mitered Borders**, page 151, to complete **pillow top**.
2. Follow **Quilting**, page 151, to mark, layer, and quilt using **Quilting Diagram**, page 60, as a suggestion. Our pillow tops are hand quilted.
3. Follow **Pillow Finishing**, page 158, to complete pillows with welting.

BLESSED NATION SAMPLER

The simple images and inspiring words of this quilted sampler reflect the ideals on which our nation evolved — home, liberty, brotherhood, and faith. Fused to the pieced center panel are provincial designs that include rustic cabins, golden stars, a flag, and a trio of friends. All the motifs are fast and easy to appliqué using heavy-duty fusible web, so there's no need to stitch around the pieces! Uniting the appliqués is a verse from Psalm 33:12, which is "stitched" using a permanent pen. The wall hanging is completed with a dogtooth border and in-the-ditch machine quilting.

BLESSED NATION SAMPLER

SKILL LEVEL: 1 2 3 4 5
WALL HANGING SIZE: 23" x 32"

YARDAGE REQUIREMENTS

Yardage is based on 45"w fabric.

☐ ¼ yd of cream print

■ ¼ yd of red plaid

◨ scraps of assorted cream prints for background

◣ scraps of assorted prints and plaids for
   appliqués and pieced squares
   1 yd for backing and hanging sleeve
   ½ yd for binding
   27" x 36" batting

You will also need:
   heavy-duty paper-backed fusible web
   black permanent fabric marker

CUTTING OUT THE PIECES

All measurements include a ¼" seam allowance. Follow
Rotary Cutting, page 144, to cut fabric.

1. **From cream print:** ☐
   - Cut 1 strip 5¾"w. From this strip, cut 5
     squares 5¾" x 5¾". Cut squares twice
     diagonally to make 20 **triangles**.

2. **From red plaid:** ■
   - Cut 1 strip 5¾"w. From this strip, cut 4
     squares 5¾" x 5¾". Cut squares twice
     diagonally to make 16 **triangles**.
   - Cut 2 squares 5⅜" x 5⅜". Cut squares once
     diagonally to make 4 **corner triangles**.

3. **From scraps of assorted cream prints for**
   background: ◨
   - Cut 1 **A** 4½" x 9".
   - Cut 1 **B** 4½" x 10".
   - Cut 1 **C** 3" x 13½".
   - Cut 1 **D** 5½" x 18½".
   - Cut 1 **E** 3" x 8".
   - Cut 1 **F** 3" x 11".
   - Cut 1 **G** 5" x 7¼".
   - Cut 1 **H** 5" x 11¾".
   - Cut 1 **I** 3" x 18½".
   - Cut 1 **J** 5¼" x 13½".
   - Cut 1 **K** 5¼" x 5½".

4. **From scraps of assorted prints and plaids:** ◣
   - Cut 23 **squares** 1¾" x 1¾".

PREPARING THE APPLIQUÉS

*Referring to photo and **Wall Hanging Top Diagram**,*
*follow **Preparing Fusible Appliqués**, page 149, to cut*
pieces from scraps using patterns, pages 68 - 69, and
indicated measurements.

1 **flag pole** — ½" x 11¾"	1 **heart**
1 **flag stars** — 1⅞" x 2"	1 **banner**
2 **flag stripes** — ½" x 3⅞"	5 **stars**
2 **flag stripes** — ½" x 5¾"	3 **tree tops**
3 **tree trunks** — ½" x ¾"	3 **tree centers**
3 **houses** — 3" x 3⅜"	3 **tree bottoms**
3 **chimneys** — ¾" x ¾"	3 **roofs**
3 **doors** — 1" x 2¼"	3 **house sides**
4 **windows** — 1" x 1"	1 **tulip**
1 **sunflower**	1 **tulip stem**
1 **sunflower center**	1 **violet**
1 **sunflower stem**	1 **violet center**
1 **shirt**	1 **violet stem**
2 **dresses**	3 **bodies**
1 **boy hair piece**	1 **pants**
2 **girl hair pieces**	

ASSEMBLING THE WALL HANGING TOP

*Follow **Piecing and Pressing**, page 146, to make wall*
hanging top.

1. Sew 8 **squares** together to make **Unit 1**. Sew 15
   squares together to make **Unit 2**.

Unit 1 (make 1)

Unit 2 (make 1)

2. Referring to **Assembly Diagram**, sew **Unit 1**,
   Unit 2, and pieces **A - K** together into rows. Sew
   rows together, trimming short edges of **Unit 2**
   even with raw edges of row above to make
   center section of wall hanging top.
3. Sew 7 **triangles** together to make **Top/Bottom
   Border**. Make 2 **Top/Bottom Borders**. Sew 11
   triangles together to make **Side Border**. Make
   2 **Side Borders**.

Top/Bottom Border (make 2)

Side Border (make 2)

4. Referring to **Wall Hanging Top Diagram**, sew **Top**, **Bottom**, and **Side Borders** to center section. Sew 1 **corner triangle** to each corner of center section.

5. Use permanent marker to write "Ps 33:12" on banner; use dashed lines to write "Blessed is the nation whose God is the Lord" on wall hanging top.

6. Follow manufacturer's instructions to fuse appliqués to center section to complete **Wall Hanging Top**.

COMPLETING THE WALL HANGING

1. Follow **Quilting**, page 151, to layer and quilt. Our wall hanging is machine quilted in the ditch along seamlines.

2. Follow **Making a Hanging Sleeve**, page 157, to attach hanging sleeve to wall hanging.

3. Follow **Binding**, page 155, to bind wall hanging using 1¾"w straight-grain binding with mitered corners.

Assembly Diagram

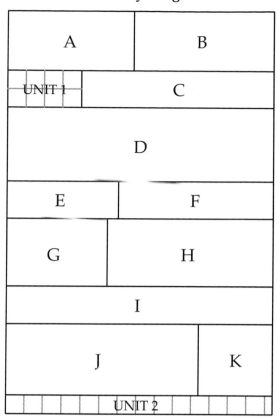

Wall Hanging Top Diagram

Tulip

Tulip Stem

Roof

House Side

Sunflower

Violet Center

Violet

Sunflower Center

Violet Stem

Sunflower Stem

Tree Bottom

Tree Top

Tree Center

68

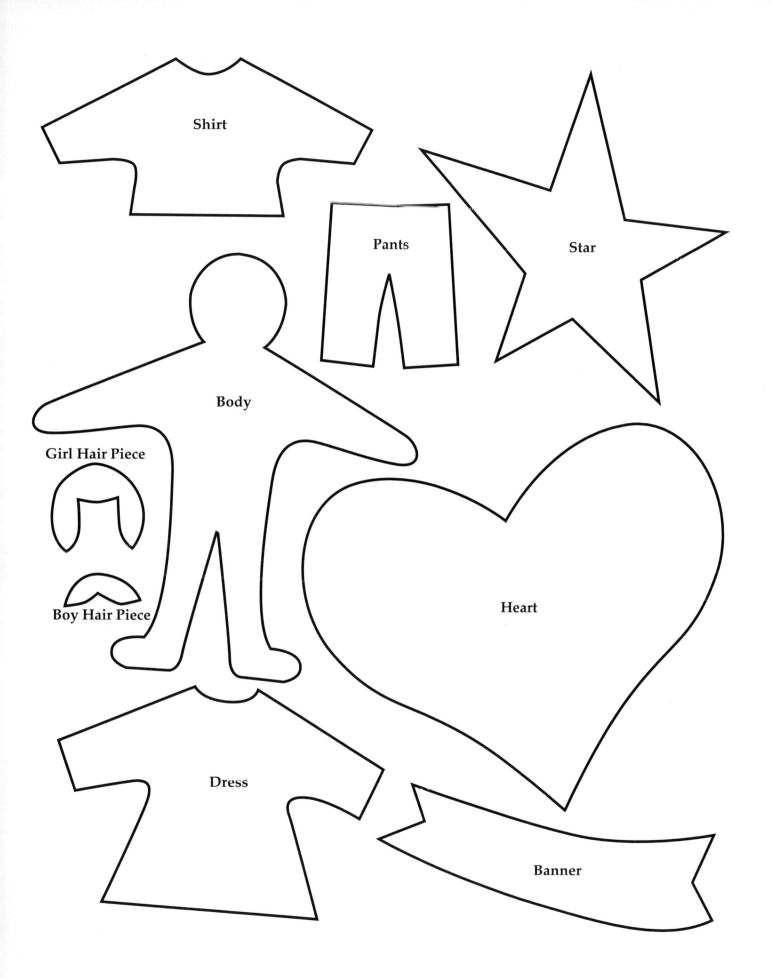

Shirt

Pants

Star

Body

Girl Hair Piece

Boy Hair Piece

Heart

Dress

Banner

FASHION FIREWORKS

You'll be decked out in all-American style when you don these dressed-up duds! In just a few simple steps, purchased garments can be transformed into one-of-a-kind originals using fabric scraps and eye-catching motifs. For a star-spangled skirt and blouse, just cut a variety of fabric pieces and fuse them in place. Primitive stars, colorful buttons, and a matching sash complete the country look. It's also fun to "recycle" a flea market find into a trendy accessory. Simply add patriotic motifs to patchwork panels, which are then fused onto the front of a men's vest. Machine stitched with clear nylon thread, the appliqués finish the vest with Fourth of July flair.

A quilter who's always on the go will love our star-struck tote (below). It's great for keeping portable projects close at hand! The ready-made bag features a fused-on block with four easy-to-piece Variable Stars. Turn an ordinary knit top into a patriotic pullover (opposite) by adding a grosgrain ribbon streamer and starry appliqués. So easy to create, the accents are fused in place and secured with topstitching.

VICTORY VEST

Our instructions provide general guidelines for piecing the rectangles of fabric to cover the front of a purchased vest. We encourage you to use different appliqués or leftover pieced blocks from other projects to create your own special design.

SUPPLIES

Yardage is based on 45"w fabric.

- a men's suit vest (we found ours at a resale shop)
- 1½ yds *total* of assorted cream print fabrics for vest fronts
- scraps of assorted fabrics for appliqués
- paper-backed fusible web
- transparent monofilament thread for appliqué
- tracing paper
- assorted buttons

MAKING THE VEST

1. Remove buttons from vest. Use seam ripper to take vest apart at shoulder and side seams. Set aside vest back.
2. To make patterns, place right vest front piece, right side up, on tracing paper. Use a pencil to draw around vest front piece; draw a second line ¼" outside the first. Cut out along outer line and label pattern. Repeat for left vest front piece.
3. To cover vest front pieces, use cream print fabrics and follow **Rotary Cutting**, page 144, and **Piecing and Pressing**, page 146, to piece a rectangle large enough for *each* pattern piece. Our rectangles were pieced using 5½"l pieces with widths varying from 2" to 5" (**Fig. 1**).

Fig. 1

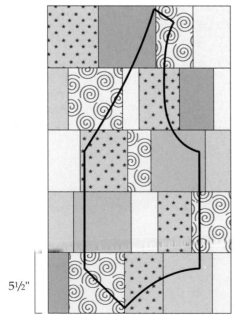

5½"

4. Place patterns, right side down, on wrong side of pieced rectangles; cut out.
5. Referring to photo, use desired patterns, pages 78 and 79, and follow **Preparing Fusible Appliqués**, page 149, to cut out appliqués from scraps. Follow **Invisible Appliqué**, page 149, to stitch appliqués to pieced vest fronts.
6. To prepare pieced vest fronts, draw a third line ¼" inside first line on tracing paper patterns. Cut out along innermost line to make pattern for web. Place patterns, right side down, on paper backing side of web. Draw around each pattern and cut out. Center 1 web shape on wrong side of each pieced vest front; fuse in place. Remove paper backing.
7. For each vest front, center pieced vest front, right side up, on right side of original vest front (fabric will extend ¼" past vest edges); fuse in place.
8. Press raw edges of each pieced vest front under ¼" so that pressed edges match edges of original vest fronts. Topstitch in place through all layers.
9. To reassemble vest, refer to **Fig. 2** and insert shoulder and side seam allowances of vest front pieces between lining and outer fabric of vest back at shoulder and side seams. Topstitch through all layers.

Fig. 2

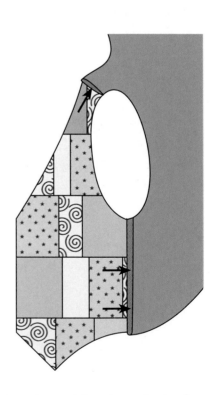

10. Sew buttons to vest fronts as desired.

STAR-SPANGLED COORDINATES

SUPPLIES

a cotton skirt and blouse
fat quarters (18" x 22" pieces) and/or scraps
   of assorted blue, red, and gold print fabrics
   for appliqués
assorted buttons
transparent monofilament thread for appliqué
paper-backed fusible web

TRIMMING THE SKIRT AND BLOUSE

1. Wash, dry, and press garments and fabrics.
2. Use pattern, page 79, and follow **Preparing Fusible Appliqués**, page 149, to cut desired number of extra-large star appliqués and rectangular patches from scraps. (Our patches are cut 5½"l with widths varying from 2" to 5".)
3. Referring to photo, follow **Invisible Appliqué**, page 149, to stitch appliqués to skirt and blouse, overlapping and staggering appliqués as desired.
4. Remove buttons from blouse. Replace with buttons of same size.
5. Sew additional buttons to centers of star appliqués.
6. (*Note:* For Steps 6 and 7, follow **Rotary Cutting**, page 144, and **Piecing and Pressing**, page 146.) To make belt, measure waistline and add 36". Cut belt pieces 5½"l with widths varying from 2" to 9". Sew belt pieces together along 5½"l edges to achieve determined measurement (**Fig. 1**).

Fig. 1

5½"

7. Matching right sides, press belt in half lengthwise. Sew raw edges together, leaving a 6" opening for turning. Cut corners diagonally, turn right side out, and press. Blindstitch opening closed.

PATRIOTIC PULLOVER

SUPPLIES

a pullover top
1"w navy grosgrain ribbon
scraps of gold print fabric for appliqués
transparent monofilament thread for appliqué
paper-backed fusible web

TRIMMING THE PULLOVER

1. Wash, dry, and press top, fabric, and ribbon.
2. Draw a straight vertical line on top front beginning 1¼" from neck opening (**Fig. 1**).

Fig. 1

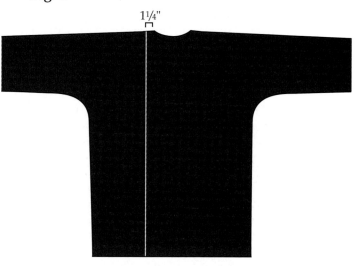

1¼"

3. Cut a length of ribbon 3" longer than drawn line. Follow manufacturer's instructions to fuse web to wrong side of ribbon.
4. Use patterns, page 79, and follow **Preparing Fusible Appliqués**, page 149, to cut 2 large stars, 2 medium stars, and 2 small stars from scraps.
5. Center ribbon along drawn line; pin in place. Use seam ripper to open shoulder seam as far as necessary to insert top end of ribbon into seam. Turn lower end of ribbon to wrong side of top and pin.
6. Follow manufacturer's instructions to fuse ribbon to top. Stitch shoulder seam closed along previous seamline. Topstitch along edges of ribbon.
7. Referring to photo, follow **Invisible Appliqué**, page 149, to stitch stars to top.

TOTE BAG

BLOCK SIZE: 11" x 11"

SUPPLIES

a canvas tote bag large enough to accommodate an 11" x 11" design

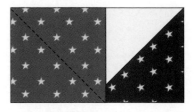 1 fat quarter (18" x 22" piece) *each* of cream print and blue print fabrics

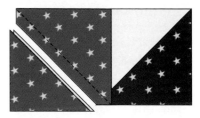 scraps of red and blue print fabrics
paper-backed fusible web

CUTTING OUT THE PIECES

All measurements include a 1/4" seam allowance. Follow **Rotary Cutting**, *page 144, to cut fabric.*

1. **From cream print fabric:** ☐
   - Cut 17 **squares** 1½" x 1½".
   - Cut 16 **rectangles** 1½" x 2½".

2. **From blue print fabric:**
   - Cut 4 **sashing strips** 1½" x 4½".
   - Cut 2 **top/bottom borders** 1¾" x 12".
   - Cut 2 **side borders** 1¾" x 9½".

3. **From red print scraps:**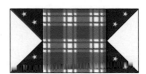
   - Cut 2 **center squares** 2½" x 2½".
   - Cut 2 sets of 8 matching **squares** 1½" x 1½".

4. **From blue print scraps:**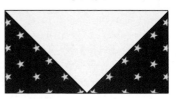
   - Cut 2 **center squares** 2½" x 2½".
   - Cut 2 sets of 8 matching **squares** 1½" x 1½".

MAKING THE TOTE BAG

Follow **Piecing and Pressing**, *page 146, to make tote bag.*

1. Place 1 **square** on 1 **rectangle** and stitch diagonally as shown in **Fig. 1**. Trim ¼" from stitching line as shown in **Fig. 2**. Press open, pressing seam allowance toward darker fabric.

Fig. 1

Fig. 2

2. Place a matching **square** on opposite end of **rectangle**. Stitch diagonally as shown in **Fig. 3**. Trim ¼" from stitching line as shown in **Fig. 4**. Press open, pressing seam allowance toward darker fabric to make **Unit 1**.

Fig. 3

Fig. 4

Unit 1

3. Repeat Steps 1 and 2 using remaining **squares** and **rectangles** to make a total of 8 **Unit 1's** using red **squares** and 8 **Unit 1's** using blue **squares**.

4. (*Note:* For Steps 4 - 6, use 4 matching **Unit 1's**.) Sew 2 cream **squares** and 1 **Unit 1** together to make **Unit 2**. Make 2 **Unit 2's**.

Unit 2 (make 2)

5. Sew 2 **Unit 1's** and 1 **center square** together to make 1 **Unit 3**.

Unit 3 (make 1)

6. Sew **Unit 2's** and **Unit 3** together to make **Unit 4**.

Unit 4

7. Referring to **Block** diagram, repeat Steps 4 - 6 to make a total of 4 **Unit 4's**.
8. Sew 2 **Unit 4's** and 1 **sashing strip** together to make **Unit 5**. Make 2 **Unit 5's**.

Unit 5 (make 2)

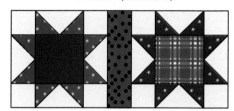

9. Sew 2 **sashing strips** and 1 **square** together to make 1 **Unit 6**.

Unit 6 (make 1)

10. Referring to **Block** diagram, sew **Unit 5's** and **Unit 6** together to make center section of block.
11. Sew **top**, **bottom**, then **side borders** to center section to complete **Block**.
12. Press raw edges of **Block** 1/2" to wrong side. Cut a 10½" x 10½" square of web. Follow manufacturer's instructions to center and fuse web to wrong side of **Block**. Remove paper backing.
13. Fuse **Block** to tote bag.
14. Topstitch along pressed edges of **Block**.

Block

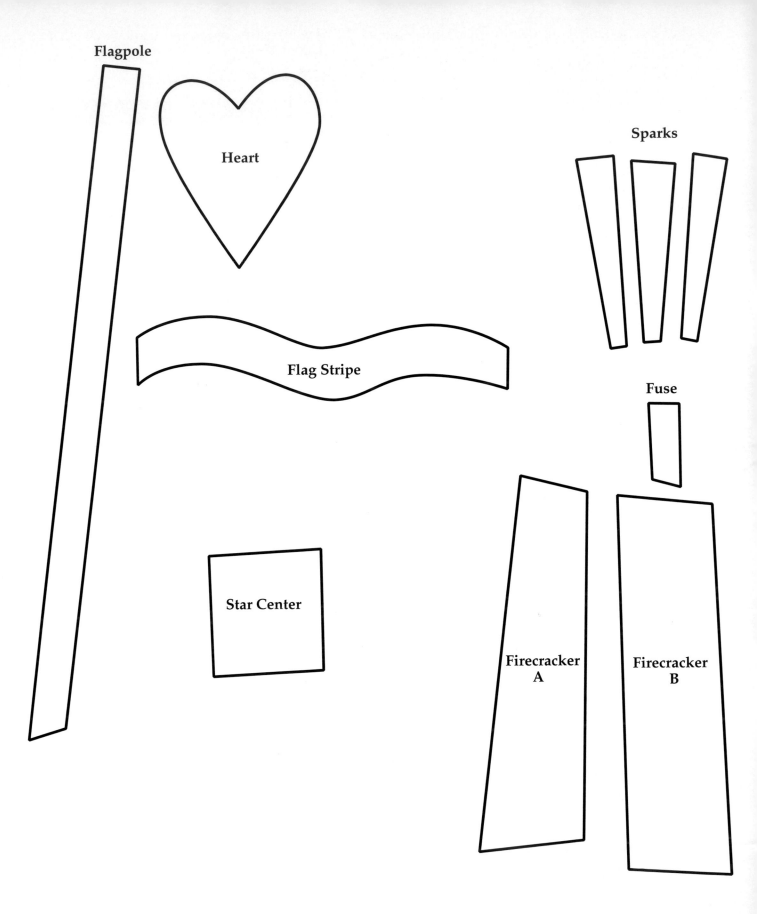

Flagpole

Heart

Sparks

Flag Stripe

Fuse

Star Center

Firecracker A

Firecracker B

Extra-Large Star

Medium Star

Large Star

Small Star

TOWN SQUARE

Continuing a time-honored tradition, life in America's heartland often revolves around a picturesque town square. The courthouse plaza, encircled by an avenue of family-owned businesses, provides a shady backdrop for gatherings such as the farmer's market, impromptu bluegrass concerts, or quilt shows. Characterizing hometown simplicity, our Town Square quilt is made using basic rotary cut pieces, so it's easy for beginners! The vibrant red center square in each block is edged by creamy white and rich navy triangles to create the look of layered squares. White borders finish the blocks and provide a pleasing contrast to the blue print sashing.

TOWN SQUARE QUILT

SKILL LEVEL: 1 2 3 4 5
BLOCK SIZE: 9¹/₂" x 9¹/₂"
QUILT SIZE: 73" x 86"

YARDAGE REQUIREMENTS

Yardage is based on 45"w fabric.

- 3¹/₈ yds of navy print for sashing and inner borders
- 2³/₄ yds of white solid
- 1¹/₄ yds *total* of assorted navy prints
- ³/₈ yd of red solid
  5¹/₄ yds for backing
  1 yd for binding
  81" x 96" batting

CUTTING OUT THE PIECES

All measurements include a ¹/₄" seam allowance. Follow Rotary Cutting, page 144, to cut fabric.

1. **From navy print for sashing and inner borders:**
   - Cut 2 lengthwise **side inner borders** 2¹/₂" x 86".
   - Cut 4 lengthwise **sashing strips** 4³/₄" x 78³/₄".
   - Cut 2 lengthwise **top/bottom inner borders** 2¹/₂" x 69".
   - From remaining fabric, cut 25 **sashing pieces** 4³/₄" x 10".

2. **From white solid:**
   - Cut 2 lengthwise **side outer borders** 2" x 90".
   - Cut 2 lengthwise **top/bottom outer borders** 2" x 73".
   - From remaining fabric, cut 6 crosswise strips 3³/₈"w. From these strips, cut 60 squares 3³/₈" x 3³/₈". Cut squares once diagonally to make 120 **triangles**.
   - From remaining fabric, cut 27 crosswise strips 1³/₄"w. From these strips, cut 60 **top/bottom block borders** 1³/₄" x 10" and 60 **side block borders** 1³/₄" x 7¹/₂".

3. **From assorted navy prints:**
   - For *each* of 30 Blocks, cut 2 matching squares 4³/₈" x 4³/₈". Cut squares once diagonally to make 4 **large triangles**.

4. **From red solid:**
   - Cut 3 strips 4"w. From these strips, cut 30 **squares** 4" x 4".

ASSEMBLING THE QUILT TOP

Follow Piecing and Pressing, page 146, to make quilt top.

1. Sew 4 **triangles** and 1 **square** together to make **Unit 1**. Make 30 **Unit 1's**.

Unit 1 (make 30)

2. Sew 4 matching **large triangles** and 1 **Unit 1** together to make **Unit 2**. Make 30 **Unit 2's**.

Unit 2 (make 30)

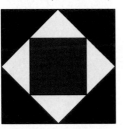

3. Sew **side**, then **top** and **bottom block borders** to **Unit 2** to make **Block**. Make 30 **Blocks**.

Block (make 30)

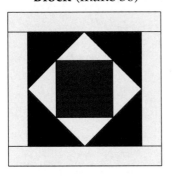

4. Referring to **Quilt Top Diagram**, sew 6 **Blocks** and 5 **sashing pieces** together to make vertical **Row**. Make 5 **Rows**.

Row (make 5)

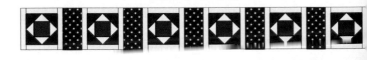

5. Referring to **Quilt Top Diagram**, sew **Rows** and **sashing strips** together to make center section of quilt top.
6. Follow **Adding Squared Borders**, page 150, to sew **top**, **bottom**, then **side inner borders** to center section. Repeat to add **outer borders** to complete **Quilt Top**.

COMPLETING THE QUILT

1. Follow **Quilting**, page 151, to mark, layer, and quilt. Our quilt is hand quilted in diagonal lines.
2. Cut a 30" square of binding fabric. Follow **Binding**, page 155, to bind quilt using 2¹/₂"w bias binding with mitered corners.

Quilt Top Diagram

COLONIAL STRIPPY COLLECTION

A trademark pattern for English and Welsh quilters in the early 1700's, the Strippy quilt was favored as an open canvas for their traditional lavish quilting designs. As immigrants from those regions settled in Pennsylvania, they introduced the distinctive pattern to pioneering Americans. The quick-to-piece tops were adapted and completed with basic quilting to create useful yet beautiful works — the same qualities that make the Strippy perfect for today's busy quilters, too! In our Colonial Strippy quilt, alternating vertical panels of red and white produce a bold patriotic look. Basic templates are used to create the geometric angles and gentle scallops in the border, providing a striking complement to the straight lines of the quilt.

A variety of colorful throw pillows will add star-spangled style to the bedroom. The star motifs in each pillow are accented with units cut from easy strip sets.

COLONIAL STRIPPY QUILT

SKILL LEVEL: 1 2 3 4 5
QUILT SIZE: 93" x 106"

YARDAGE REQUIREMENTS

Yardage is based on 45"w fabric.

■ 5¼ yds of red solid

☐ 4¼ yds of white solid

■ 2 yds of navy solid
8⅜ yds for backing
1 yd for binding
120" x 120" batting

You will also need:
plastic template material

CUTTING OUT THE PIECES

All measurements include a ¼" seam allowance.

1. Follow **Rotary Cutting**, page 144, to cut 8 lengthwise **strips** 5½" x 88½" from red solid and 7 lengthwise **strips** 5½" x 88½" from white solid. From navy solid, cut 4 **squares** 9⅛" x 9⅛".

2. To make templates for border pieces, use a permanent fine-point marker to carefully trace patterns for **A**, **B**, and **C**, page 90, onto template material. Cut out templates and check against original patterns for accuracy.

3. To cut border pieces, place templates on wrong side of fabric and use a sharp fabric marking pencil to draw around templates. Cut 40 **A's** from red solid, 74 **B's** and 8 **C's** (4 in reverse) from white solid, and 38 **A's** from navy solid.

ASSEMBLING THE QUILT TOP

*Follow **Piecing and Pressing**, page 146, to make quilt top. Refer to **Quilt Top Diagram** for color placement when making center section and borders.*

1. Sew **strips** together to make center section of quilt top.

2. Sew 9 red **A's**, 9 navy **A's**, 17 **B's**, and 2 **C's** (1 in reverse) together to make **Top Border**. Arranging colors in mirror image, repeat to make **Bottom Border**.

3. Sew 11 red **A's**, 10 navy **A's**, 20 **B's**, and 2 **C's** (1 in reverse) together to make **Side Border**. Make 2 **Side Borders**.

4. Sew 1 **square** to each end of each **Side Border**. Sew **Top**, **Bottom**, then **Side Borders** to center section. Use a compass or round object to trim corners to a rounded shape to complete **Quilt Top**.

COMPLETING THE QUILT

1. Follow **Quilting**, page 151, to mark, layer, and quilt using **Quilting Diagram** as a suggestion. Our quilt is hand quilted.

2. Cut a 28" square of binding fabric. Follow Steps 1 - 7 of **Making Continuous Bias Strip Binding**, page 155, to make 1¼"w bias binding. Press 1 long raw edge of binding ¼" to wrong side.

3. Referring to Steps 1 and 2 of **Attaching Binding with Mitered Corners**, page 156, pin binding to front of quilt, matching long raw edge of binding to scalloped edge of quilt top. Using a ¼" seam allowance and easing around curves, sew binding to quilt until binding overlaps beginning end by 2"; trim excess binding.

4. Trim batting and backing even with raw edges of quilt top. Fold pressed edge of binding to quilt back and pin in place, covering stitching line. Blindstitch binding to backing.

Quilting Diagram

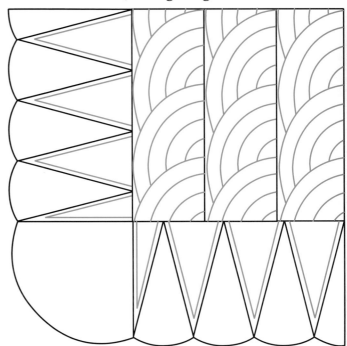

▬ ▬ ▬ ▬ ▬ ▬ ▬ ▬ ▬ ▬ ▬ ▬ QUICK TIP ▬ ▬ ▬ ▬ ▬ ▬

USING TEMPLATES ACCURATELY

Since it is occasionally necessary to use templates for cutting some pieces, the following tips will help you achieve the same accuracy with template cutting as with rotary cutting.

- *Using plastic template material (see **Quilting Supplies**, page 143) instead of cardboard will give you more accurate results, since the edges will not wear down with repeated use.*
- *When cutting out templates with straight edges, use your rotary cutter (save an old blade for this purpose) and ruler to get a perfectly straight edge.*
- *Carefully label templates with the pattern name and other pertinent information to keep from mixing them up. Store all templates for one pattern in a marked envelope.*

- *To keep templates from slipping while you draw around them, place self-adhesive sandpaper dots (available at quilt shops or from mail-order sources) on the back of each template.*
- *Placing your fabric on a non-slip surface, such as your rotary cutting mat or a sheet of sandpaper, will help you draw more accurately.*
- *When drawing around templates, use an extremely sharp pencil or a mechanical pencil with a very fine lead and draw with the pencil placed at a very low angle to the fabric. This will make a fine line and will reduce drag on the fabric, which can cause distortion.*
- *When cutting out fabric pieces, cut just inside the drawn line using very sharp scissors or, for straight edges, your rotary cutter and ruler.*

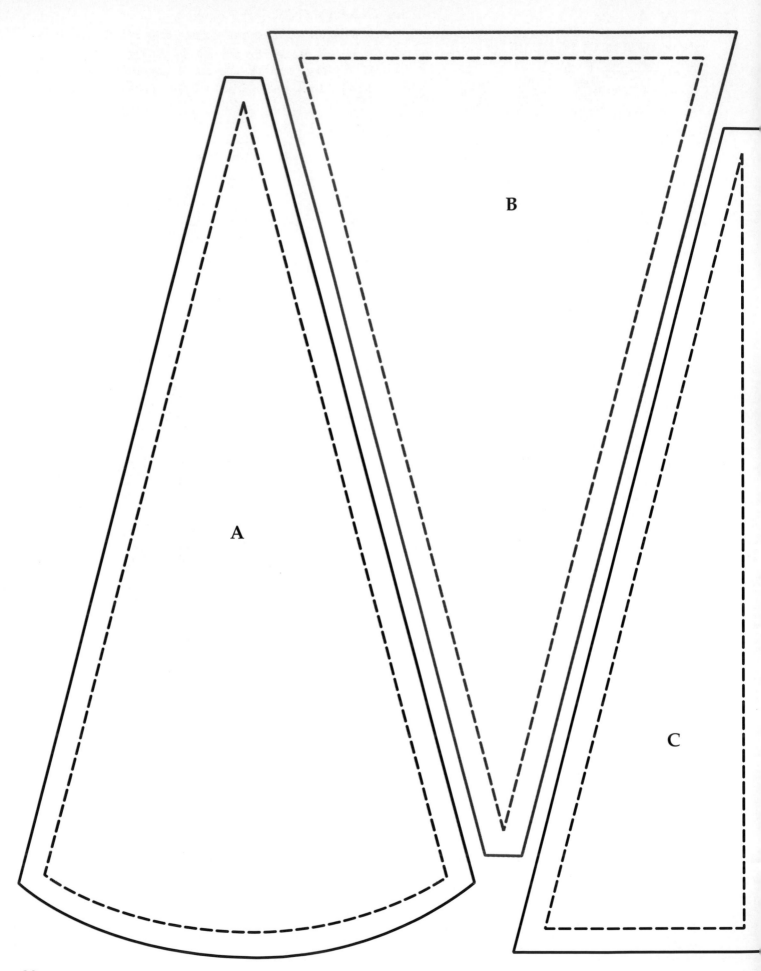

A

B

C

PILLOW A

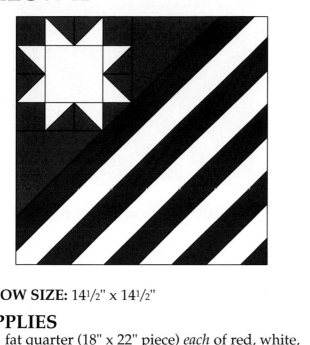

PILLOW SIZE: 14½" x 14½"

SUPPLIES

1 fat quarter (18" x 22" piece) *each* of red, white, and navy solid fabrics
18" x 18" pillow top backing fabric
15" x 15" pillow back fabric
18" x 18" batting
2 yds of 2"w bias fabric strip for welting
2 yds of ⁷/₃₂" cord for welting
polyester fiberfill
15" square rotary cutting ruler

CUTTING OUT THE PIECES

All measurements include a ¼" seam allowance. Follow Rotary Cutting, page 144, to cut fabric.

1. **From red solid:**
    - Cut 5 **strips** 1¾" x 22".

2. **From white solid:**
    - Cut 4 **strips** 1¾" x 22".
    - Cut 1 **large square** 7" x 7" for triangle-squares.
    - Cut 1 **square** 4" x 4".

3. **From navy solid:**
    - Cut 1 **large square** 7" x 7" for triangle-squares.
    - Cut 1 square 6⅛" x 6⅛". Cut square once diagonally to make 2 **large triangles**.
    - Cut 1 square 2⅝" x 2⅝". Cut square once diagonally to make 2 **small triangles**. (You will need 1 and have 1 left over.)
    - Cut 3 **small squares** 2¼" x 2¼".

MAKING PILLOW A

*Follow **Piecing and Pressing**, page 146, to make pillow.*

1. To make triangle-squares, place white and navy **large squares** right sides together. Referring to **Fig. 1**, follow **Making Triangle-Squares**, page 147, to make 8 **triangle-squares**.

Fig. 1

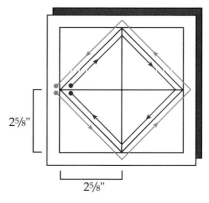

triangle-square (make 8)

2. Sew 2 **small squares** and 2 **triangle-squares** together to make 1 **Unit 1**.

Unit 1 (make 1)

3. Sew 4 **triangle-squares** and **square** together to make 1 **Unit 2**.

Unit 2 (make 1)

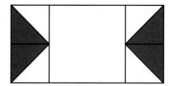

4. Sew 1 **small square**, 2 **triangle-squares**, and 1 **small triangle** together to make 1 **Unit 3**.

Unit 3 (make 1)

5. Sew **Units 1, 2,** and **3** together to make **Unit 4.**

Unit 4 (make 1)

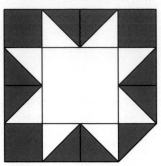

6. Sew **large triangles** and **Unit 4** together to make **Unit 5.**

Unit 5 (make 1)

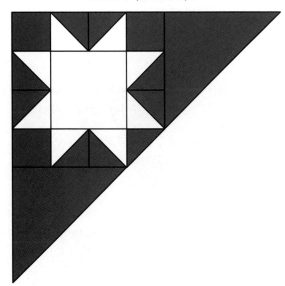

7. Sew **strips** together to make **Unit 6.**

Unit 6 (make 1)

8. Matching centers, sew long edge of **Unit 5** to 1 long edge of **Unit 6** to make **Unit 7.**

Unit 7 (make 1)

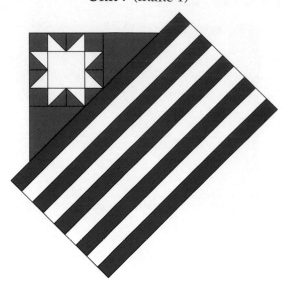

9. Using 15" square ruler, trim top and left edges of **Unit 7** even with edges of **Unit 5.** Referring to **Fig. 2**, trim **Unit 7** to a 14½" square to complete **Pillow Top A.**

Fig. 2

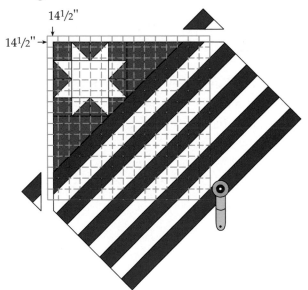

10. Follow **Quilting**, page 151, to layer and quilt in the ditch along seamlines. Our pillow top is hand quilted.
11. Trim batting and backing even with edges of pillow top.
12. Follow **Pillow Finishing**, page 158, to complete pillow with welting.

PILLOW B

PILLOW SIZE: 14¹/₂" x 14¹/₂"

SUPPLIES

1 fat quarter (18" x 22" piece) *each* of red, white, and navy solid fabrics
18" x 18" pillow top backing fabric
15" x 15" pillow back fabric
18" x 18" batting
2 yds of 2"w bias fabric strip for welting
2 yds of ⁷/₃₂" cord for welting
polyester fiberfill

CUTTING OUT THE PIECES

All measurements include a ¹/₄" seam allowance. Follow Rotary Cutting, page 144, to cut fabric.

1. **From red solid:**
   • Cut 1 **rectangle** 5" x 9" for triangle-squares.
   • Cut 4 **large rectangles** 1¹/₂" x 6¹/₂".
   • Cut 8 **small rectangles** 1¹/₂" x 2¹/₂".
   • Cut 8 **squares** 1¹/₂" x 1¹/₂".

2. **From white solid:**
   • Cut 1 **rectangle** 5" x 9" for triangle-squares.
   • Cut 4 **large rectangles** 1¹/₂" x 6¹/₂".
   • Cut 8 **small rectangles** 1¹/₂" x 2¹/₂".
   • Cut 8 **squares** 1¹/₂" x 1¹/₂".

3. **From navy solid:**
   • Cut 2 **short borders** 1¹/₂" x 12¹/₂".
   • Cut 2 **long borders** 1¹/₂" x 14¹/₂".
   • Cut 2 **rectangles** 5" x 9" for triangle-squares.
   • Cut 4 **squares** 2¹/₂" x 2¹/₂".

MAKING PILLOW B

Follow Piecing and Pressing, page 146, to make pillow.

1. To make triangle-square A's, place 1 red and 1 navy **rectangle** right sides together. Referring to **Fig. 1**, follow **Making Triangle-Squares**, page 147, to make 16 **triangle-square A's**.

Fig. 1

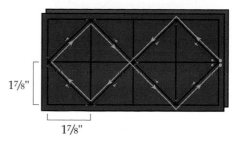

1⁷/₈"

1⁷/₈"

triangle-square A (make 16)

2. Repeat Step 1 using white and remaining navy **rectangle** to make 16 **triangle-square B's**.

triangle-square B (make 16)

3. Sew 2 **small rectangles** and 2 **triangle-square A's** together to make **Unit 1**. Make 4 **Unit 1's**.

Unit 1 (make 4)

4. Sew 2 **squares**, 1 **triangle-square A**, and 1 **triangle-square B** together to make **Unit 2**. Make 4 **Unit 2's**.

Unit 2 (make 4)

5. Sew 1 **triangle-square B**, 1 **triangle-square A**, and 2 **squares** together to make **Unit 3**. Make 4 **Unit 3's**.

Unit 3 (make 4)

6. Sew 1 **Unit 2**, 1 **square**, and 1 **Unit 3** together to make **Unit 4**. Make 4 **Unit 4's**.

Unit 4 (make 4)

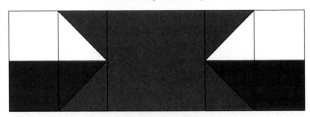

7. Sew 2 **small rectangles** and 2 **triangle-square B's** together to make **Unit 5**. Make 4 **Unit 5's**.

Unit 5 (make 4)

8. Sew 2 **large rectangles**, 1 **Unit 1**, 1 **Unit 4**, and 1 **Unit 5** together to make **Unit 6**. Make 4 **Unit 6's**.

Unit 6 (make 4)

9. Referring to **Pillow B** diagram, page 93, sew 4 **Unit 6's** together to make center section of pillow top.
10. Sew **short borders** to opposite edges of center section; sew **long borders** to remaining edges to complete **Pillow Top B**.
11. Follow **Quilting**, page 151, to layer and quilt in the ditch along seamlines. Our pillow top is hand quilted.
12. Trim batting and backing even with edges of pillow top.
13. Follow **Pillow Finishing**, page 158, to complete pillow with welting.

PILLOW C

PILLOW SIZE: 14$\frac{1}{2}$" x 14$\frac{1}{2}$"

SUPPLIES
1 fat quarter (18" x 22" piece) *each* of red, white, and navy solid fabrics
18" x 18" pillow top backing fabric
15" x 15" pillow back fabric
18" x 18" batting
2 yds of 2"w bias fabric strip for welting
2 yds of $\frac{7}{32}$" cord for welting
polyester fiberfill

CUTTING OUT THE PIECES
All measurements include a $\frac{1}{4}$" seam allowance. Follow Rotary Cutting, page 144, to cut fabric.

1. **From red solid:**
   - Cut 4 **strips** 1$\frac{3}{16}$" x 14".
   - Cut 1 square 9$\frac{1}{4}$" x 9$\frac{1}{4}$". Cut square twice diagonally to make 4 **large triangles**. (You will need 1 and have 3 left over.)
   - Cut 1 square 4$\frac{7}{8}$" x 4$\frac{7}{8}$". Cut square once diagonally to make 2 **small triangles**. (You will need 1 and have 1 left over.)

2. **From white solid:** ☐
   - Cut 1 **rectangle** 5" x 9" for triangle-squares.
   - Cut 4 **strips** 1³/₁₆" x 14".
   - Cut 1 square 9¼" x 9¼". Cut square twice diagonally to make 4 **large triangles**. (You will need 1 and have 3 left over.)
   - Cut 1 square 4⅞" x 4⅞". Cut square once diagonally to make 2 **small triangles**. (You will need 1 and have 1 left over.)
   - Cut 2 **squares** 2½" x 2½".

3. **From navy solid:** ■
   - Cut 1 **rectangle** 5" x 9" for triangle-squares.
   - Cut 2 squares 4⅞" x 4⅞". Cut squares once diagonally to make 4 **small triangles**.
   - Cut 2 **short borders** 1½" x 12½".
   - Cut 2 **long borders** 1½" x 14½".
   - Cut 8 **small squares** 1½" x 1½".

MAKING PILLOW C
*Follow **Piecing and Pressing**, page 146, to make pillow top.*

1. To make triangle-squares, place white and navy **rectangles** right sides together. Referring to **Fig. 1**, follow **Making Triangle-Squares**, page 147, to make 16 **triangle-squares**.

Fig. 1

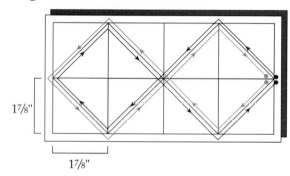

17/8"

17/8"

triangle-square (make 16)

2. Sew 2 **small squares** and 2 **triangle-squares** together to make **Unit 1**. Make 4 **Unit 1's**.

Unit 1 (make 4)

3. Sew 4 **triangle-squares** and 1 **square** together to make **Unit 2**. Make 2 **Unit 2's**.

Unit 2 (make 2)

4. Sew 2 **Unit 1's** and 1 **Unit 2** together to make **Unit 3**. Make 2 **Unit 3's**.

Unit 3 (make 2)

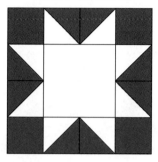

5. Sew **strips** together to make **Strip Set**. Place **Strip Set** on cutting mat with red **strip** at bottom. To make first cut, place rotary cutting ruler on **Strip Set** as shown in **Fig. 2** with 45° marking (shown in pink) aligned with bottom edge. Make cut.

Fig. 2

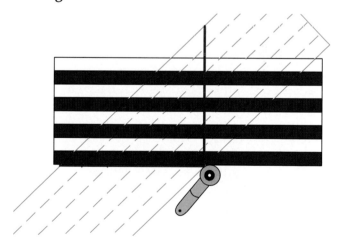

6. To make second cut, turn **Strip Set** 180° on mat. Align previously cut 45° edge of **Strip Set** with 4½" marking on ruler (**Fig. 3**) and make cut to complete **Unit 4**.

Fig. 3

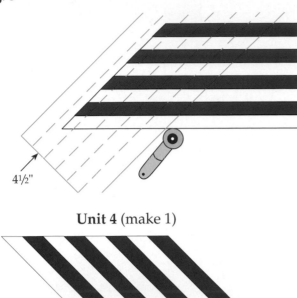

Unit 4 (make 1)

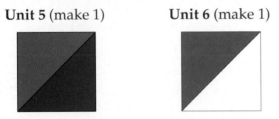

7. Sew 2 **small triangles** together to make 1 **Unit 5**. Sew 2 **small triangles** together to make 1 **Unit 6**.

Unit 5 (make 1)   Unit 6 (make 1)

8. Sew **Unit 5**, 1 **Unit 3**, and 1 **small triangle** together to make 1 **Unit 7**.

Unit 7 (make 1)

9. Sew 1 **small triangle**, 1 **Unit 3**, and **Unit 6** together to make 1 **Unit 8**.

Unit 8 (make 1)

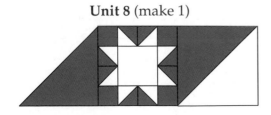

10. Referring to **Fig. 4**, sew **Unit 4** and **Unit 8** together, ending stitching ¼" from inside corner and backstitching. Sew **Unit 7** and **Unit 4** together, ending stitching ¼" from inside corner and backstitching to make **Unit 9**.

Fig. 4

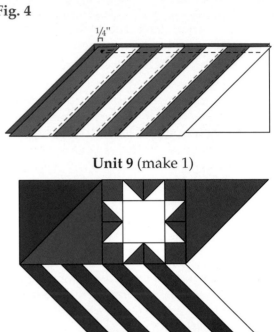

Unit 9 (make 1)

11. Referring to **Pillow C** diagram, page 94, follow Steps 2 - 4 of **Working with Diamonds and Set-in Seams**, page 148, to sew **large triangles** and **Unit 9** together to make center section of pillow top.
12. Sew **short borders** to opposite edges of center section; sew **long borders** to remaining edges to complete **Pillow Top C**.
13. Follow **Quilting**, page 151, to layer and quilt in the ditch along seamlines. Our pillow top is hand quilted.
14. Trim batting and backing even with edges of pillow top.
15. Follow **Pillow Finishing**, page 158, to complete pillow with welting.

PILLOW D

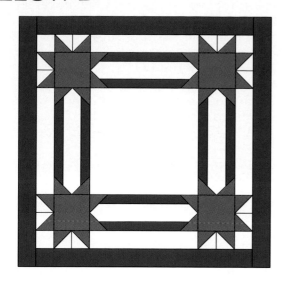

PILLOW SIZE: 15" x 15"

SUPPLIES

 1 fat quarter (18" x 22" piece) *each* of red, white, and navy solid fabrics
19" x 19" pillow top backing fabric
15¹/₂" x 15¹/₂" pillow back fabric
19" x 19" batting
2 yds of 2"w bias fabric strip for welting
2 yds of ⁷/₃₂" cord for welting
polyester fiberfill

CUTTING OUT THE PIECES

All measurements include a ¹/₄" seam allowance. Follow Rotary Cutting, page 144, to cut fabric.

1. **From red solid:** ▮
   • Cut 4 **strips** 1" x 22".
   • Cut 2 **short borders** 1³/₄" x 12¹/₂".
   • Cut 2 **long borders** 1³/₄" x 15".

2. **From white solid:** ☐
   • Cut 2 **strips** 1¹/₂" x 22".
   • Cut 1 **large rectangle** 5" x 9" for triangle-squares.
   • Cut 1 **large square** 6¹/₂" x 6¹/₂".
   • Cut 4 **rectangles** 1¹/₂" x 6¹/₂".
   • Cut 4 **small squares** 1¹/₂" x 1¹/₂".

3. **From navy solid:** ▮
   • Cut 1 **large rectangle** 5" x 9" for triangle-squares.
   • Cut 4 **squares** 2¹/₂" x 2¹/₂".
   • Cut 16 **small squares** 1¹/₂" x 1¹/₂".

MAKING PILLOW D

Follow Piecing and Pressing, page 146, to make pillow.

1. Using white and navy **large rectangles**, follow Step 1 of **Making Pillow C**, page 95, to make 16 **triangle-squares**.

2. Sew 2 **triangle-squares** together to make **Unit 1**. Make 8 **Unit 1's**.

Unit 1 (make 8)

3. Sew 1 **small square**, 2 **Unit 1's**, and 1 **square** together to make **Unit 2**. Make 4 **Unit 2's**.

Unit 2 (make 4)

4. Sew **strips** together to make **Strip Set**. Make 2 **Strip Sets**. Cut across **Strip Sets** at 6¹/₂" intervals to make 4 **Unit 3's**.

Strip Set (make 2)   **Unit 3** (make 4)

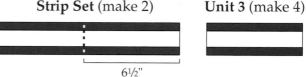

6¹/₂"

5. Place 1 **small square** on 1 corner of 1 **Unit 3** and stitch diagonally (**Fig. 1**). Trim ¹/₄" from stitching line (**Fig. 2**). Press open, pressing seam allowance toward blue fabric.

Fig. 1

Fig. 2

97

6. Repeat Step 5 on each remaining corner of **Unit 3** to complete **Unit 4**. Make 4 **Unit 4's**.

Unit 4 (make 4)

7. Sew 1 **Unit 4** and 1 **rectangle** together to make **Unit 5**. Make 4 **Unit 5's**.

Unit 5 (make 4)

8. Sew 2 **Unit 2's** and 1 **Unit 5** together to make **Unit 6**. Make 2 **Unit 6's**.

Unit 6 (make 2)

9. Sew 2 **Unit 5's** and **large square** together to make **Unit 7**.

Unit 7 (make 1)

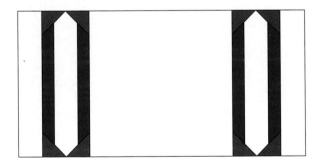

10. Referring to **Pillow D** diagram, page 97, sew **Unit 6's** and **Unit 7** together to make center section of pillow top.
11. Sew **short borders** to opposite edges of center section; sew **long borders** to remaining edges to complete **Pillow Top D**.
12. Follow **Quilting**, page 151, to layer and quilt in the ditch along seamlines. Our pillow top is hand quilted.
13. Trim batting and backing even with edges of pillow top.
14. Follow **Pillow Finishing**, page 158, to complete pillow with welting.

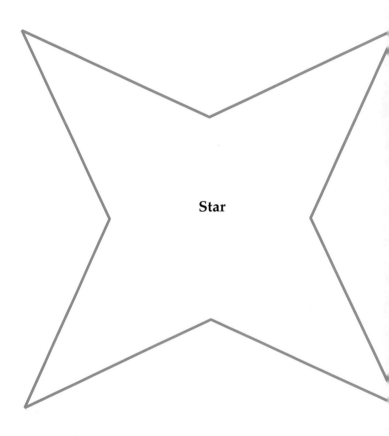

Star

PILLOW E

PILLOW SIZE: 14$\frac{1}{2}$" x 14$\frac{1}{2}$"

SUPPLIES

- 1 fat quarter (18" x 22" piece) *each* of red, white, and navy solid fabrics
- 18" x 18" pillow top backing fabric
- 15" x 15" pillow back fabric
- 18" x 18" batting
- 2 yds of 2"w bias fabric strip for welting
- 2 yds of $\frac{7}{32}$" cord for welting
- polyester fiberfill
- 10" x 15" piece of white organdy or other very lightweight cotton fabric
- transparent monofilament thread for appliqué

CUTTING OUT THE PIECES

All measurements include a $\frac{1}{4}$" seam allowance. Follow Rotary Cutting, page 144, to cut fabric.

1. **From red solid:**
   - Cut 2 **strips** 2" x 22".
   - Cut 2 **short borders** 1$\frac{1}{2}$" x 12$\frac{1}{2}$".
   - Cut 2 **long borders** 1$\frac{1}{2}$" x 14$\frac{1}{2}$".
2. **From white solid:**
   - Cut 1 **strip** 1$\frac{1}{2}$" x 22".
   - Cut 1 **piece** 10" x 15" for star appliqués.
3. **From navy solid:**
   - Cut 5 **squares** 4$\frac{1}{2}$" x 4$\frac{1}{2}$".

MAKING PILLOW E

Follow Piecing and Pressing, page 146, to make pillow.

1. Sew **strips** together to make **Strip Set**. Cut across **Strip Set** at 4$\frac{1}{2}$" intervals to make 4 **Unit 1's**.

Strip Set (make 1)   **Unit 1** (make 4)

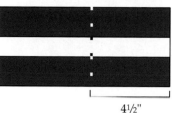

4$\frac{1}{2}$"

2. Use pattern, page 98, to trace 5 **stars** onto wrong side of organdy **piece**, leaving at least $\frac{1}{2}$" between drawn stars. Place organdy and white solid **pieces** right sides together and stitch on marked line around each star. Cut out stars $\frac{1}{4}$" outside stitching line. Trim seam allowance to $\frac{1}{8}$" at star points and clip inside corners. To make an opening for turning, cut a slit in organdy only; turn right side out and press to make **star appliqué**. Make 5 **star appliqués**.
3. To make **Unit 2**, center **star appliqué** on navy **square** and follow **Mock Hand Appliqué**, page 150, to stitch around edges of star. Make 5 **Unit 2's**.

Unit 2 (make 5)

4. Referring to **Pillow E** diagram, sew **Unit 1's** and **Unit 2's** together into rows, then sew rows together to make center section of pillow top.
5. Sew **short borders** to opposite edges of center section; sew **long borders** to remaining edges to complete **Pillow Top E**.
6. Follow **Quilting**, page 151, to layer and quilt in the ditch along seamlines. Our pillow top is hand quilted.
7. Trim batting and backing even with edges of pillow top.
8. Follow **Pillow Finishing**, page 158, to complete pillow with welting.

AUNT LUCINDA'S CHAIN

Adventurous quilters have always taken great pride in designing unique patterns that reflect their personal tastes and abilities. Often these quilts have become the trademarks of their makers and serve as endearing remembrances when presented to family members. We can almost imagine how thrilled a dear niece must have been to receive a treasure (such as the one shown here) from her beloved Aunt Lucinda, for whom this masterful pattern is named. To simplify this antique quilt, we used strip piecing to create the Four-Patch units that are the basis for the pattern. Octagonal blocks formed with those units are joined with plain setting squares to produce the quilt's distinctive chain design

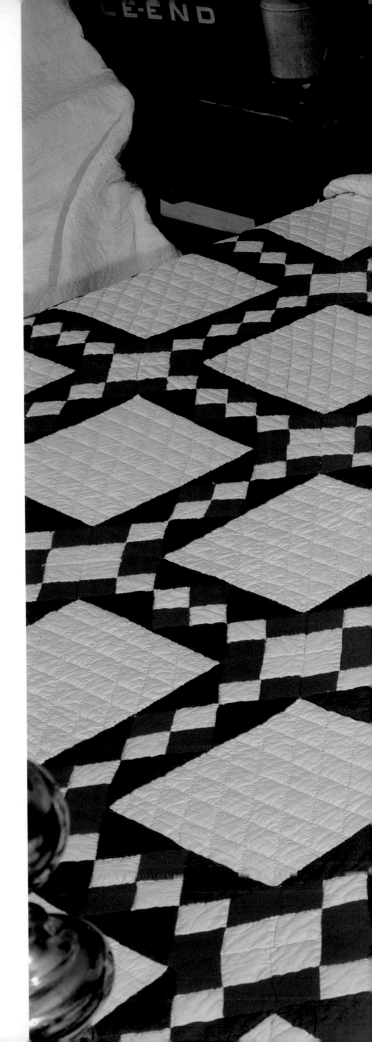

AUNT LUCINDA'S CHAIN QUILT

SKILL LEVEL: 1 2 3 4 5
BLOCK SIZE: 17" x 17"
QUILT SIZE: 77" x 89"

Our original quilt was bound by turning a folded edge of the border to the backing and hand stitching it in place. Our instructions, however, call for a more durable bias binding.

YARDAGE REQUIREMENTS
Yardage is based on 45"w fabric.

- ■ $4^1/8$ yds of red solid
- □ $3^5/8$ yds of white solid
- ■ $2^1/8$ yds of blue solid
  $5^1/2$ yds for backing
  1 yd for binding
  90" x 108" batting

CUTTING OUT THE PIECES
All measurements include a $^1/4$" seam allowance. Follow Rotary Cutting, page 144, to cut fabric.

1. **From red solid:**
   - Cut 21 **strips** 2"w.
   - Cut 2 lengthwise **side borders** $4^1/4$" x 92".
   - Cut 2 lengthwise **top/bottom borders** $4^1/4$" x 72".

2. **From white solid:**
   - Cut 21 **strips** 2"w.
   - Cut 8 strips 9"w. From these strips, cut 30 **squares** 9" x 9".

3. **From blue solid:**
   - Cut 11 strips $5^1/2$"w. From these strips, cut 76 squares $5^1/2$" x $5^1/2$". Cut squares twice diagonally to make 304 **triangles**. (You will need 302 and have 2 left over.)
   - Cut 2 squares $5^1/8$" x $5^1/8$". Cut squares once diagonally to make 4 **corner triangles**.

ASSEMBLING THE QUILT TOP
Follow Piecing and Pressing, page 146, to make quilt top.

1. Sew 2 **strips** together to make **Strip Set**. Make 21 **Strip Sets**. Cut across **Strip Sets** at 2" intervals to make 426 **Unit 1's**.

Strip Set (make 21)   **Unit 1** (make 426)

2. Sew 2 **Unit 1's** together to make **Unit 2**. Make 213 **Unit 2's**.

Unit 2 (make 213)

3. Sew 1 **triangle** and 1 **Unit 2** together to make **Unit 3**. Make 213 **Unit 3's**.

Unit 3 (make 213)

4. Sew 1 **triangle** and 1 **Unit 3** together to make **Unit 4**. Make 71 **Unit 4's**.

Unit 4 (make 71)

5. Sew 2 **Unit 3's** and 1 **Unit 4** together to make **Unit 5**. Make 71 **Unit 5's**.

Unit 5 (make 71)

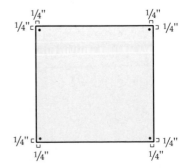

6. Referring to **Fig. 1**, mark a small dot $^1/4$" from each corner on wrong side of each **square** for stitching guides.

Fig. 1

7. Backstitching at beginning and ending of seam, sew 1 **square** and 1 **Unit 5** together between dots (**Fig. 2**). Repeat to add 1 **Unit 5** to each remaining edge of **square**.

Fig. 2

8. To complete stitching at corners, fold 1 corner of **square** diagonally with right sides together and matching edges of **Unit 5's**. Stitch from end of previous stitching to outside edge, backstitching at beginning of seam (**Fig. 3**).

Fig. 3

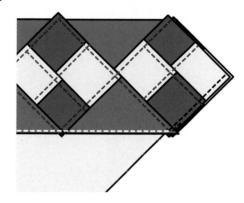

9. Repeat Step 8 for each remaining corner to complete **Block**.

Block

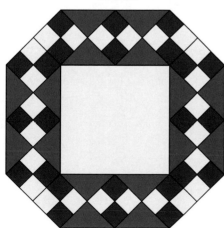

10. Repeat Steps 7 - 9 to make a total of 15 **Blocks**.

11. Referring to Step 7, sew 1 **Unit 5** and 1 **square** together, then add 2 **triangles** to make **Side Unit**. Make 7 **Side Units**.

Side Unit (make 7)

12. Referring to Steps 7 and 8, sew 1 **Unit 5** each to 2 adjacent sides of 1 **square**. Add 2 **triangles** and 1 **corner triangle** to make **Corner Unit**. Make 2 **Corner Units**.

Corner Unit (make 2)

13. Referring to **Assembly Diagram**, page 104, sew **Blocks** together into diagonal **Rows**, beginning and ending seams exactly 1/4" from each corner and backstitching at beginning and end of seam.
14. Referring to Steps 2 - 4 of **Working with Diamonds and Set-in Seams**, page 148, and **Assembly Diagram**, sew **Rows**, **Side Units**, **Corner Units**, remaining **squares**, and remaining **corner triangles** together to make center section of quilt top.
15. Follow **Adding Squared Borders**, page 150, to sew **top**, **bottom**, then **side borders** to center section to complete **Quilt Top**.

COMPLETING THE QUILT

1. Follow **Quilting**, page 151, to mark, layer, and quilt using **Quilting Diagram**, page 105, as a suggestion. Our quilt is hand quilted.
2. Cut a 32" square of binding fabric. Follow **Binding**, page 155, to bind quilt using 2¹/₂"w bias binding with mitered corners.

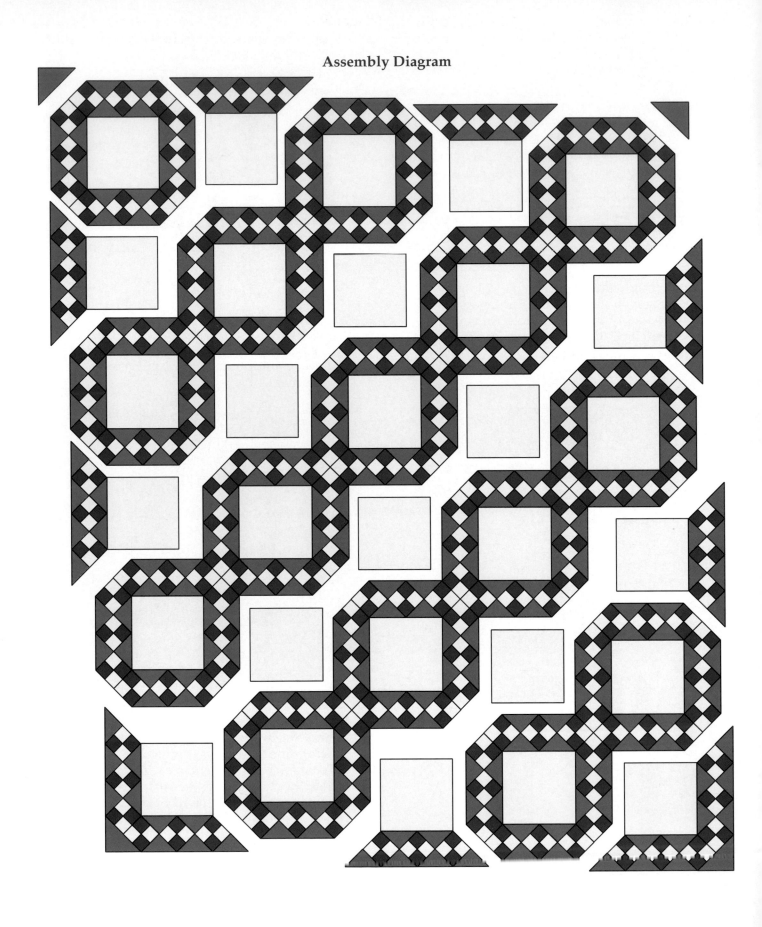

Quilt Top Diagram

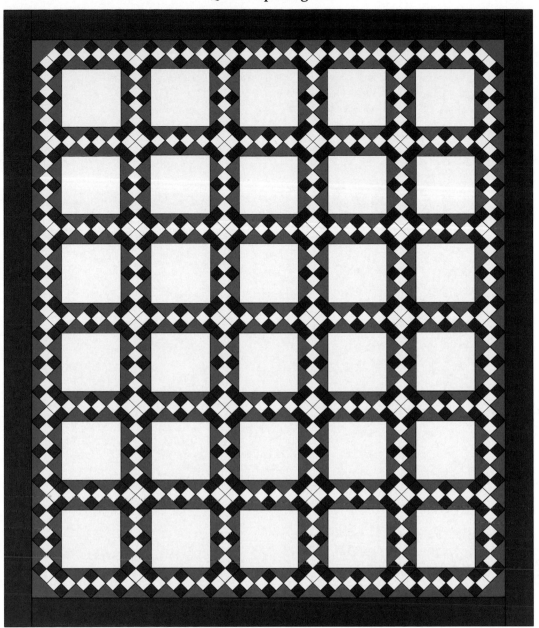

Quilting Diagram

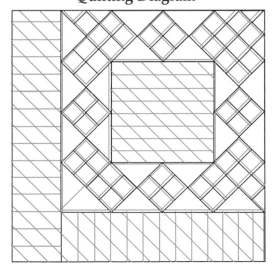

CENTENNIAL MEDALLION COLLECTION

Cherished as masterpiece quilts in the 1700's, medallion designs regained prestige in the next century as the United States celebrated its centennial anniversary in 1876. Quilters honored their forefathers and expressed their patriotism with ornate patterns such as our grand Centennial Medallion quilt. Appliquéd on its center panel are the laurels of a Revolutionary victory — golden stars, regal plumes, and sprays of flowers. These motifs are easily fused in place and machine stitched with clear nylon thread. Sawtooth and ribbon borders, simplified by speed-piecing techniques, are encircled by a handsome appliquéd outer border. Emblems of freedom, majestic eagles accent the pillow flip

Create matching accents using motifs from the Centennial Medallion quilt. Our winning window treatment (below) is easy to make using grid-pieced sawtooth borders and a blue ribbon border. Finished with a simple blue welted edging, the valance is complemented by sawtooth curtain tiebacks. To make a generous wall hanging (opposite), we replaced the corner flowers in the quilt's center panel with a quartet of valiant eagle appliqués. A patriotic pillow is crafted with four golden pieced stars.

109

CENTENNIAL MEDALLION QUILT

SKILL LEVEL: 1 2 3 4 5
QUILT SIZE: 89" x 105"

YARDAGE REQUIREMENTS

Yardage is based on 45"w fabric.

- 8³/₈ yds of white print
- 2¹/₄ yds of red print
- 2¹/₄ yds of blue print
- 1 yd of dark blue print
- ¹/₂ yd of gold print
- ¹/₄ yd of dark gold print
- ¹/₄ yd of brown print
- ¹/₄ yd of green print
- ¹/₄ yd of rust print
  8¹/₄ yds for backing
  1 yd for binding
  120" x 120" batting

You will also need:
  paper-backed fusible web
  transparent monofilament thread for appliqué

CUTTING OUT THE PIECES

All measurements include a ¹/₄" seam allowance. Follow Rotary Cutting, page 144, to cut fabric.

1. **From white print:**
   - Cut 4 lengthwise **border pieces** 9¹/₂" x 69¹/₂".
   - Cut 1 strip 8¹/₂"w. From this strip, cut 4 **corner squares** 8¹/₂" x 8¹/₂".
   - Cut 15 strips 2¹/₂"w. From these strips, cut 238 **small squares** 2¹/₂" x 2¹/₂".
   - Cut 8 **rectangles** 13" x 22" for triangle-squares.
   - Cut 4 **large squares** 25¹/₂" x 25¹/₂".
   - From remaining fabric width, cut 1 lengthwise **pillow flip** 15¹/₂" x 85¹/₂".
   - Cut 4 squares 3¹/₄" x 3¹/₄". Cut squares twice diagonally to make 16 **triangles**.

2. **From red print:**
   - Cut 8 **rectangles** 13" x 22" for triangle-squares.

3. **From blue print:**
   - Cut 4 strips 6¹/₂"w. From these strips, cut 52 **rectangles** 2¹/₂" x 6¹/₂".

4. **From dark blue print:**
   - Cut 4 strips 6¹/₂"w. From these strips, cut 52 **rectangles** 2¹/₂" x 6¹/₂".

5. **From gold print:**
   - Cut 1 **strip** 1¹/₂"w.

6. **From dark gold print:**
   - Cut 1 **strip** 1¹/₂"w.

PREPARING THE APPLIQUÉS

*Referring to **Quilt Top Diagram**, use patterns, pages 117 - 119, and follow **Preparing Fusible Appliqués**, page 149, to cut the following pieces from remaining fabric:*

16 **flowers**	2 **heads** (1 in reverse)
32 **leaves**	2 **tails** (1 in reverse)
8 **stems** — ³/₈" x 11¹/₂"	4 **wings** (2 in reverse)
4 **stems** — ³/₈" x 10¹/₂"	2 **shields**
4 **stems** — ³/₈" x 8¹/₂"	2 **shield tops**
56 gold **stars**	4 **arrow shafts**
3 blue **stars**	4 **arrowheads**
40 **swags** (20 in reverse)	

ASSEMBLING THE QUILT TOP

*Follow **Piecing and Pressing**, page 146, to make quilt top.*

1. Referring to **Quilt Top Diagram**, page 113, sew **large squares** together to make **medallion background**.
2. Referring to photo and **Quilt Top Diagram**, page 113, follow **Invisible Appliqué**, page 149, to stitch appliqués to **medallion background** to make **Medallion**, to **border pieces** to make **Appliquéd Borders**, and to **pillow flip**.
3. Carefully trim **Medallion** to 48¹/₂" x 48¹/₂", **Appliquéd Borders** to 8¹/₂" x 68¹/₂", and **pillow flip** to 14¹/₂" x 84¹/₂".
4. To make triangle-squares, place 1 red and 1 white **rectangle** right sides together. Referring to **Fig. 1**, follow **Making Triangle-Squares**, page 147, to make 56 **triangle-squares**. Repeat with remaining **rectangles** to make a total of 448 **triangle-squares**.

Fig. 1

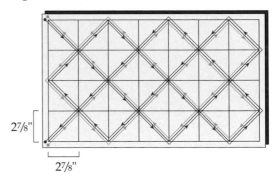

2⁷/₈"   2⁷/₈"

triangle-square (make 448)

5. (*Note:* For Steps 5 - 8, refer to **Quilt Top Diagram**, page 113.) Sew 24 **triangle-squares** together to make **First Sawtooth Border** (inner border). Make 4 **First Sawtooth Borders**.
6. Sew 32 **triangle-squares** together to make **Second Sawtooth Border**. Make 4 **Second Sawtooth Borders**.
7. Sew 42 **triangle-squares** together to make **Third** and **Top Sawtooth Borders**. Make 4 **Third Sawtooth Borders** and 1 **Top Sawtooth Border**.

- Sew 7 **triangle-squares** together to make **Short Sawtooth Border**. Make 2 **Short Sawtooth Borders**.
- With right sides together, place 1 **small square** on each end of 1 dark blue **rectangle**. Referring to **Fig. 2**, stitch diagonally across squares. Trim ¼" from stitching line and press toward darker fabric to make **Unit 1**. Make 52 **Unit 1's**.

Fig. 2   **Unit 1** (make 52)

0. Using **small squares** and blue **rectangles** and stitching in the opposite direction (**Fig. 3**), repeat Step 9 to make 52 **Unit 2's**.

Fig. 3   **Unit 2** (make 52)

1. Sew 1 **Unit 1** and 1 **Unit 2** together to make **Unit 3**. Make 52 **Unit 3's**.

Unit 3 (make 52)

2. Sew 13 **Unit 3's** together to make **Ribbon Border**. Make 4 **Ribbon Borders**.

Ribbon Border (make 4)

3. To cut parallelograms for stars, place gold and dark gold **strips** right sides together, carefully matching raw edges. Referring to **Fig. 4**, align 45° marking (shown in pink) on rotary cutting ruler with lower edges of **strips**. Cut along right edge of ruler to cut 1 end of **strips** at a 45° angle.

Fig. 4

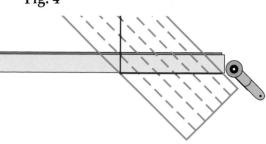

14. Turn cut **strips** 180° and align 45° marking on rotary cutting ruler with lower edges of **strips**. Align previously cut 45° edge with 2½" marking on ruler. Cut at 2½" intervals as shown in **Fig. 5** to cut 16 pairs of **parallelograms**.

Fig. 5

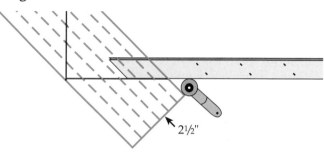

2½"

15. (*Note:* For Steps 15 - 18, follow **Working with Diamonds and Set-in Seams**, page 148.) Sew 1 pair of **parallelograms** together to make **Unit 4**. Make 16 **Unit 4's**.

Unit 4 (make 16)

16. Sew 2 **Unit 4's** together to make **Unit 5**. Make 8 **Unit 5's**.

Unit 5 (make 8)

17. Sew 2 **Unit 5's** together to make **Unit 6**. Make 4 **Unit 6's**.

Unit 6 (make 4)

18. Sew 1 **Unit 6**, 4 **triangles**, and 4 **small squares** together to make **Star Block**. Make 4 **Star Blocks**.

Star Block (make 4)

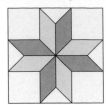

19. (*Note:* For Steps 19 - 25, refer to **Quilt Top Diagram**.) Sew 1 **First Sawtooth Border** each to opposite edges of **Medallion**. Sew 1 **small square** to each end of each remaining **First Sawtooth Border**; sew borders to remaining edges of **Medallion**.
20. Sew 1 **Ribbon Border** each to opposite edges of **Medallion**. Sew 1 **Star Block** to each end of each remaining **Ribbon Border**; sew borders to remaining edges of **Medallion**.
21. Sew 1 **Second Sawtooth Border** each to opposite edges of **Medallion**. Sew 1 **small square** to each end of each remaining **Second Sawtooth Border**; sew borders to remaining edges of **Medallion**.

22. Sew 1 **Appliquéd Border** each to opposite edges of **Medallion**. Sew 1 **corner square** to each end of each remaining **Appliquéd Border**; sew borders to remaining edges of **Medallion**.
23. Sew 1 **Third Sawtooth Border** each to opposite edges of **Medallion**. Sew 1 **small square** to each end of each remaining **Third Sawtooth Border**; sew borders to remaining edges of **Medallion**.
24. Sew 1 **Short Sawtooth Border** to each end of **pillow flip**; sew **pillow flip** to top edge of **Medallion**.
25. Sew 1 **small square** to each end of **Top Sawtooth Border**. Sew border to top edge of **pillow flip** to complete **Quilt Top**.

COMPLETING THE QUILT
1. Follow **Quilting**, page 151, to mark, layer, and quilt using **Quilting Diagram** as a suggestion. Our quilt is hand quilted.
2. Cut a 34" square of binding fabric. Follow **Binding**, page 155, to bind quilt using $2^1/2$"w bias binding with mitered corners.

Quilting Diagram

EAGLE MEDALLION WALL HANGING

SKILL LEVEL: 1 2 3 4 5
WALL HANGING SIZE: 69" x 69"

YARDAGE REQUIREMENTS
Yardage is based on 45"w fabric.

- [ ] 4¼ yds of white print
- ■ 1¾ yds of red print
- ■ 1⅜ yds of blue print
- ■ 1 yd of dark blue print
- ■ ⅜ yd of brown print
- ▢ ¼ yd of gold print
- ■ ¼ yd of rust print
- ▢ ⅛ yd of dark gold print
- ■ ⅛ yd of green print
  4½ yds for backing and hanging sleeve
  ⅞ yd for binding
  72" x 72" batting

You will also need:
  paper-backed fusible web
  transparent monofilament thread for appliqué

CUTTING OUT THE PIECES
All measurements include a ¼" seam allowance. Follow Rotary Cutting, page 144, to cut fabric.

1. **From white print:** ▢
   - Cut 14 strips 2½"w. From these strips, cut 232 **small squares** 2½" x 2½".
   - Cut 4 **large squares** 25½" x 25½".
   - From remaining fabric width, cut 4 **rectangles** 13" x 22" for triangle-squares.
   - Cut 4 squares 3¼" x 3¼". Cut squares twice diagonally to make 16 **triangles**.

2. **From red print:** ■
   - Cut 4 **rectangles** 13" x 22" for triangle-squares.

3. **From blue print:** ■
   - Cut 4 strips 6½"w. From these strips, cut 52 **rectangles** 2½" x 6½".

4. **From dark blue print:** ■
   - Cut 4 strips 6½"w. From these strips, cut 52 **rectangles** 2½" x 6½".

5. **From gold print:** ▢
   - Cut 1 **strip** 1½"w.

6. **From dark gold print:** ■
   - Cut 1 **strip** 1½"w.

PREPARING THE APPLIQUÉS
Referring to photo, use patterns, pages 117 - 119, and follow Preparing Fusible Appliqués, page 149, to cut the following pieces from remaining fabric:

4 **flowers**	4 **tails**
8 **leaves**	4 **shields**
4 **stems** — ⅜" x 8½"	4 **shield tops**
8 gold **stars**	8 **arrow shafts**
5 blue **stars**	8 **arrowheads**
4 **heads**	8 **swags** (4 in reverse)
8 **wings** (4 in reverse)	

ASSEMBLING THE WALL HANGING TOP
Follow Piecing and Pressing, page 146, to make wall hanging top. Instructions refer to Assembling the Quilt Top for Centennial Medallion Quilt, page 110.

1. Referring to **Wall Hanging Top Diagram**, sew 4 **large squares** together to make **medallion background**.
2. Referring to photo and **Wall Hanging Top Diagram**, follow **Invisible Appliqué**, page 149, to stitch appliqués to **medallion background** to make **Medallion**.
3. Carefully trim **Medallion** to 48½" x 48½".
4. Refer to Step 4, page 110, to make a total of 224 **triangle-squares**.
5. Follow Steps 5 and 6, page 110, to make **First** and **Second Sawtooth Borders**.
6. Follow Steps 9 - 12, page 111, to make 4 **Ribbon Borders**.
7. Follow Steps 13 - 18, page 111, to make 4 **Star Blocks**.
8. Follow Steps 19 - 21, page 112, to sew **Borders** to **Medallion** to complete **Wall Hanging Top**.

COMPLETING THE WALL HANGING
1. Follow **Quilting**, page 151, to mark, layer, and quilt using **Quilting Diagram**, page 112, as a suggestion. Our wall hanging is hand quilted.
2. Follow **Making a Hanging Sleeve**, page 157, to add hanging sleeve to wall hanging.
3. Cut a 28" square of binding fabric. Follow **Binding**, page 155, to bind wall hanging using 2½"w bias binding with mitered corners.

PATRIOTIC PILLOW

PILLOW SIZE: 14" x 14"

YARDAGE REQUIREMENTS

Yardage is based on 45"w fabric.

- ¼ yd of white print
- ⅛ yd *each* of blue print, gold print, and dark gold print
- 1¾ yds of 2¼"w bias strip for welting
- 1¾ yds of ¼" cord for welting
- ½ yd for pillow back

You will also need:
  polyester fiberfill

CUTTING OUT THE PIECES

All measurements include a ¼" seam allowance. Follow Rotary Cutting, page 144, to cut fabric.

1. **From white print:** ☐
    - Cut 1 strip 2½"w. From this strip, cut 16 **small squares** 2½" x 2½".
    - Cut 4 squares 3¼" x 3¼". Cut squares twice diagonally to make 16 **triangles**.

2. **From blue print:** ◼
    - Cut 4 **borders** 1½" x 12½".

3. **From gold print:** ☐
    - Cut 1 **strip** 1½"w.

4. **From dark gold print:** ◼
    - Cut 1 **strip** 1½"w.
    - Cut 4 **corner squares** 1½" x 1½".

MAKING THE PILLOW

Follow Piecing and Pressing, page 146, to make pillow.

1. Follow Steps 13 - 18 of **Assembling the Quilt Top**, page 111, to make 4 **Star Blocks**.
2. Referring to photo, sew **Star Blocks** together to make center section of pillow top.
3. Sew 1 **border** each to top and bottom edges of center section. Sew 1 **corner square** to each end of remaining borders; sew borders to side edges of center section to complete **Pillow Top**.
4. Follow **Pillow Finishing**, page 158, to complete pillow with welting.

VALANCE

VALANCE SIZE: 14" x 48"

Our valance will fit a window approximately 36"w.

YARDAGE REQUIREMENTS

Yardage is based on 45"w fabric.

- ■ 1¹/₂ yds of dark blue print
- □ ⁷/₈ yd of white print
- ■ ¹/₂ yd of red print
- ■ ¹/₄ yd of blue print
  1¹/₂ yds for backing
  3 yds of 2¹/₄"w bias strip for welting
  3 yds of ⁵/₁₆" cord for welting
  1¹/₂ yds of fusible fleece

CUTTING OUT THE PIECES

All measurements include a ¹/₄" seam allowance. Follow Rotary Cutting, page 144, to cut fabric.

1. **From dark blue print:** ■
   - Cut 2 lengthwise **border strips** 2³/₄" x 48¹/₂".
   - From remaining fabric width, cut 1 crosswise strip 6¹/₂"w. From this strip, cut 12 **rectangles** 2¹/₂" x 6¹/₂".

2. **From white print:** □
   - Cut 3 strips 2¹/₂"w. From these strips, cut 48 **small squares** 2¹/₂" x 2¹/₂".
   - Cut 2 **rectangles** 10" x 13" for triangle-squares.

3. **From red print:** ■
   - Cut 2 **rectangles** 10" x 13" for triangle-squares.

4. **From blue print:** ■
   - Cut 1 strip 6¹/₂"w. From this strip, cut 12 **rectangles** 2¹/₂" x 6¹/₂".

ASSEMBLING THE VALANCE TOP

Follow Piecing and Pressing, page 146, to make valance.

1. Follow Steps 9 - 11 of **Assembling the Quilt Top**, page 111, to make 12 **Unit 3's**. (You will need 12 **Unit 1's** and 12 **Unit 2's**.)
2. Referring to photo, sew **Unit 3's** together to make **Row**.
3. To make triangle-squares, place 1 red and 1 white **rectangle** right sides together. Referring to **Fig. 1**, follow **Making Triangle-Squares**, page 147, to make 24 **triangle-squares**. Repeat with remaining **rectangles** to make a total of 48 **triangle-squares**.

Fig. 1

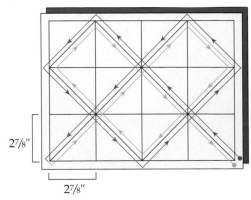

2⁷/₈"

2⁷/₈"

triangle-square (make 48)

4. Referring to photo, sew 24 **triangle-squares** together to make **pieced border**. Make 2 **pieced borders**.
5. Referring to photo, sew **pieced borders**, then **border strips** to long edges of **Row** to complete **Valance Top**.

COMPLETING THE VALANCE

1. Follow Step 2 of **Adding Welting to Pillow Top**, page 158, to make welting with a ¹/₂" seam allowance. Cut 2 pieces of welting 48¹/₂"l.
2. Matching raw edges, baste welting to top and bottom edges of valance top, using a ¹/₂" seam allowance.
3. Cut fusible fleece ¹/₂" smaller on all sides than valance top. Follow manufacturer's instructions to center and fuse fleece to wrong side of valance top.
4. Cut valance backing same size as valance top. Stitching as close as possible to welting, sew valance top and backing together along top and bottom edges.

5. Press all raw edges at open ends of valance 1/4" to wrong side. Turn valance right side out. To form rod pockets, stitch in the ditch between pieced borders and border strips. Stitch through all layers along sides, leaving ends of border strips open (**Fig. 2**).

Fig. 2

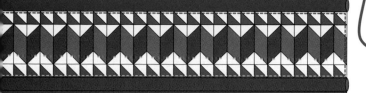

CURTAIN TIEBACKS

TIEBACK SIZE: 2 1/2" x 24 1/2"

Instructions are for making 2 tiebacks.

SUPPLIES

1 rectangle 10" x 13" *each* of red print and white print
3/8 yd of 45"w fabric for backing
3 1/2 yds of 2"w bias strip for welting
3 1/2 yds of 7/32" cord for welting
1/4 yd of fusible fleece
4 small cabone (drapery) rings

MAKING THE TIEBACKS

All measurements include a 1/4" seam allowance. Follow **Rotary Cutting**, *page 144, to cut fabric. Follow* **Piecing and Pressing**, *page 146, to make tiebacks.*

1. Refer to Step 3 of **Assembling the Valance**, page 116, to make 24 **triangle-squares**.
2. Sew 12 **triangle-squares** together to make each tieback top.

Tieback Tops

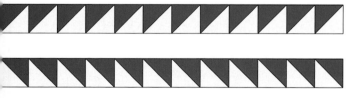

3. Follow Step 2 of **Adding Welting to Pillow Top**, page 158, to make welting. Cut welting into 2 equal lengths.
4. Follow Steps 3 and 4 of **Adding Welting to Pillow Top** to baste welting to each tieback top.

5. Cut backing same size as each tieback top. Stitching as close as possible to welting and leaving an opening for turning, sew each tieback top and backing together. Cut corners diagonally.
6. Cut fusible fleece 1/4" smaller on all sides than each tieback top. Follow manufacturer's instructions to center and fuse fleece to wrong side of each tieback top.
7. Turn tiebacks right side out; press. Blindstitch openings closed.
8. Sew 1 ring to back at each end of tiebacks.

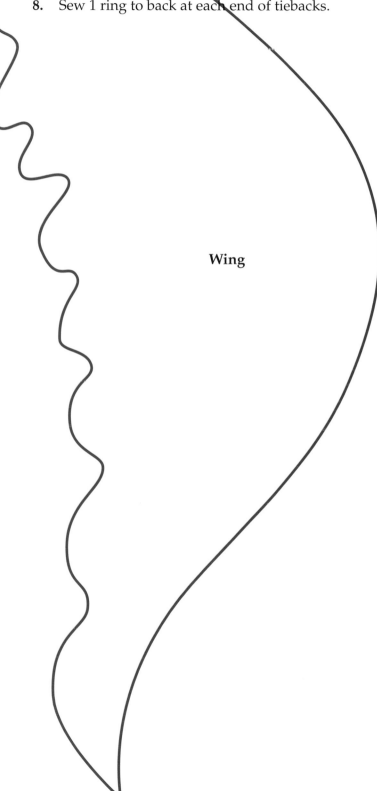

Wing

117

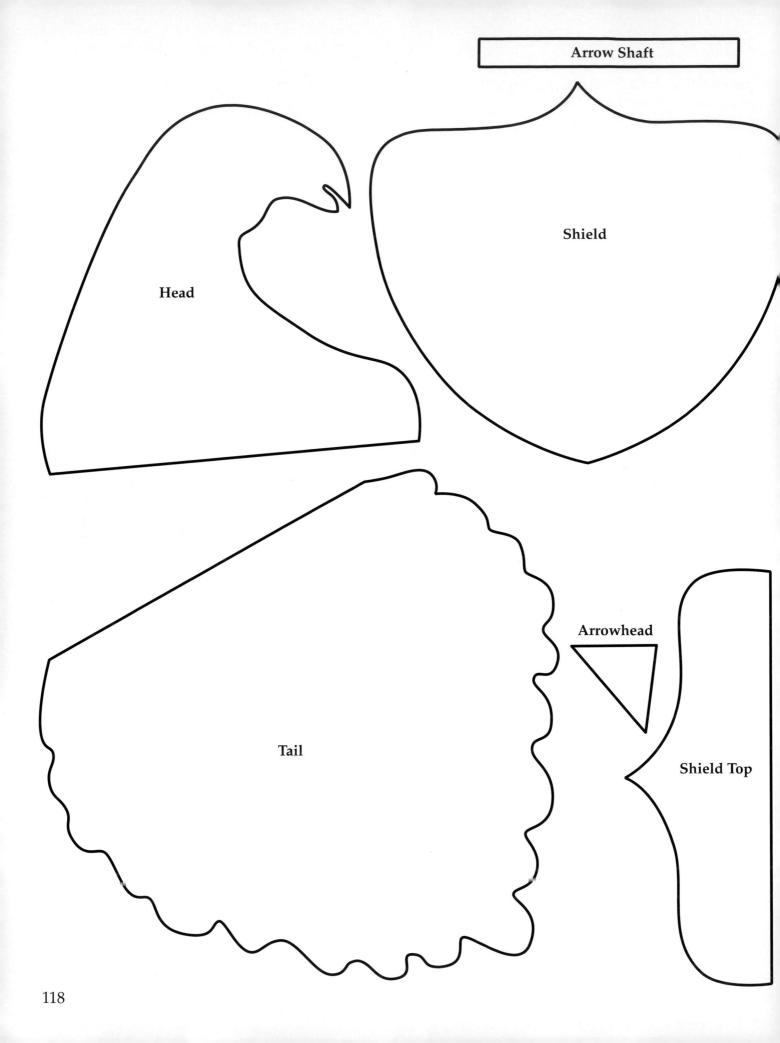

Arrow Shaft

Shield

Head

Tail

Arrowhead

Shield Top

118

Leaves

Star

Swag

Flower

TUMBLING STARS

One simple shape — the diamond — is the foundation for this intriguing pattern, which is traditionally known as Tumbling Blocks or Building Blocks. For our variation, we grouped the dark color values to produce a host of six-pointed stars. The result is a fascinating optical illusion: at first glance you might see all red and blue stars, but take another look and you'll find stars of red and white as well as blue and white! It's easy to make the diamond pieces without templates — simply align the fabric strips with the angle guides on your rotary cutting ruler and trim! We even show you how to assemble the blocks using half diamonds, eliminating the awkward set-in seams. For a grand finish, quick-pieced strip sets create a bold tri-color border.

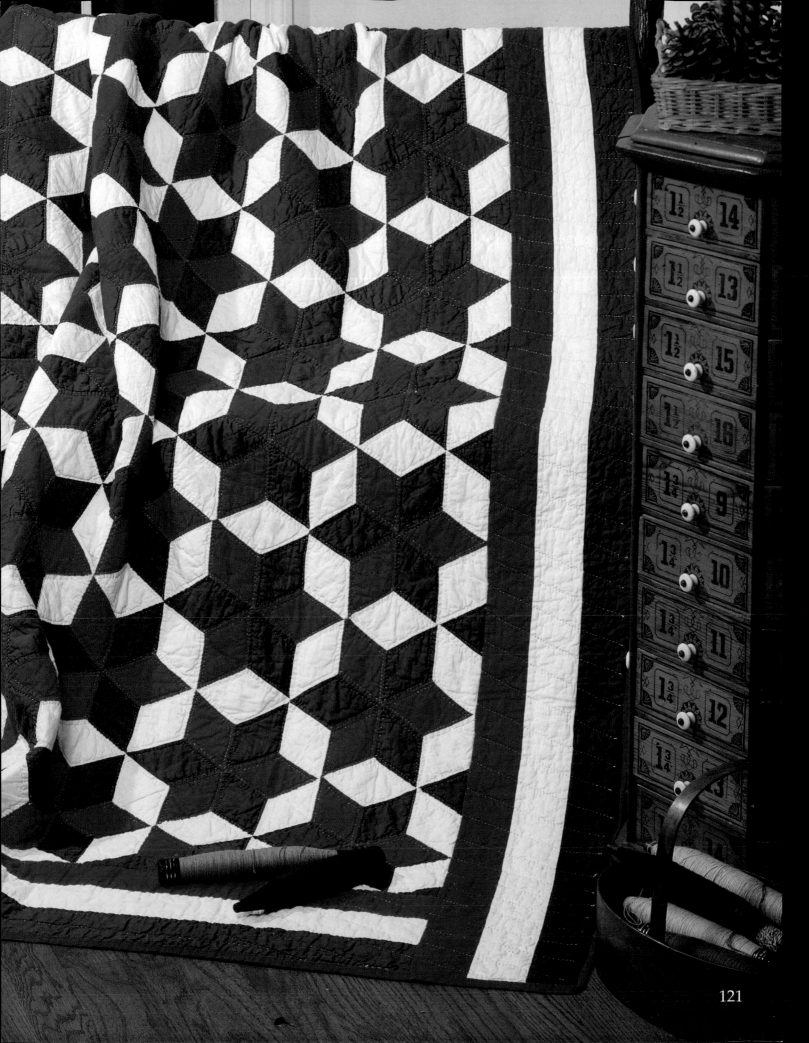

TUMBLING STARS QUILT

SKILL LEVEL: 1 2 3 4 5
QUILT SIZE: 71" x 85"

YARDAGE REQUIREMENTS

Yardage is based on 45"w fabric.

■ 2³/₄ yds of red solid

☐ 2³/₄ yds of white solid

■ 2³/₄ yds of blue solid
  5¹/₄ yds for backing
  1 yd for binding
  81" x 96" batting

CUTTING OUT THE PIECES

All measurements include a ¹/₄" seam allowance. Follow Rotary Cutting, page 144, to cut fabric.

1. **From red solid:**
   - Cut 2 lengthwise **side borders** 3" x 88".
   - Cut 2 lengthwise **top/bottom borders** 3" x 59".
   - From remaining fabric, cut 26 crosswise **strips** 3"w.

2. **From white solid:** ☐
   - Cut 2 lengthwise **side borders** 3" x 88".
   - Cut 2 lengthwise **top/bottom borders** 3" x 59".
   - From remaining fabric, cut 28 crosswise **strips** 3"w.

3. **From blue solid:** ■
   - Cut 2 lengthwise **side borders** 3" x 88".
   - Cut 2 lengthwise **top/bottom borders** 3" x 59".
   - From remaining fabric, cut 27 crosswise **strips** 3¹/₄"w.

ASSEMBLING THE QUILT TOP

Follow Piecing and Pressing, page 146, to make quilt top.

1. Referring to **Fig. 1**, align 60° marking (shown in yellow) on ruler with lower edge of 1 red **strip**. Cut along right side of ruler to cut 1 end of strip at a 60° angle.

Fig. 1

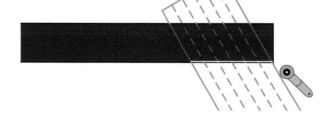

2. Turn cut **strip** 180° on mat and align 60° marking on ruler with lower edge of strip. Align previously cut 60° edge with 3" marking on ruler. Cut strip at 3" intervals as shown in **Fig. 2** to cut **diamonds**.

Fig. 2

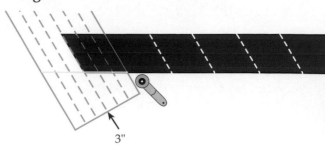

3"

3. Repeat Steps 1 and 2 with remaining red and white **strips** to cut a total of 177 **red diamonds** and 196 **white diamonds**.

red diamond (cut 177)   **white diamond** (cut 196)

4. Cutting diamonds at 3¹/₄" intervals, repeat Steps 1 and 2 with blue **strips** to cut 187 diamonds. Referring to **Fig. 3**, cut across diamonds to make a total of 374 **triangles**.

Fig. 3   **triangle** (make 374)

5. Sew 2 **diamonds** and 1 **triangle** together to make **Unit 1**. Make 59 **Unit 1's**.

Unit 1 (make 59)

6. Sew 1 **diamond** and 2 **triangles** together to make **Unit 2**. Make 59 **Unit 2's**.

Unit 2 (make 59)

7. Sew 2 **diamonds** and 1 **triangle** together to make **Unit 3**. Make 68 **Unit 3's**.

Unit 3 (make 68)

8. Sew 1 **diamond** and 2 **triangles** together to make **Unit 4**. Make 60 **Unit 4's**.

Unit 4 (make 60)

9. Sew 1 **Unit 1** and 1 **Unit 2** together to make **Unit 5**. Make 59 **Unit 5's**.

Unit 5 (make 59)

10. Sew 1 **Unit 3** and 1 **Unit 4** together to make **Unit 6**. Make 60 **Unit 6's**.

Unit 6 (make 60)

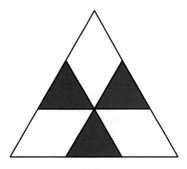

11. Referring to **Assembly Diagram**, page 124, sew **triangles**, **Unit 3's**, **Unit 5's**, and **Unit 6's** into vertical rows; sew rows together.
12. To trim top and bottom edges straight, refer to **Fig. 4** to line up ¹⁄₄" marking on ruler (shown in yellow) with seam intersections. Trim off excess to make center section of quilt top.

Fig. 4

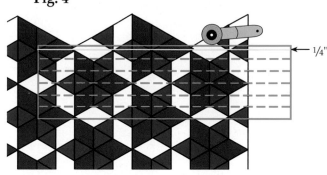

←— ¹⁄₄"

13. Sew 1 each of red, white, and blue **top/bottom borders** together to make **Top/Bottom Border Unit**. Make 2 **Top/Bottom Border Units**. Repeat with **side borders** to make 2 **Side Border Units**.

Border Unit

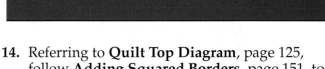

14. Referring to **Quilt Top Diagram**, page 125, follow **Adding Squared Borders**, page 151, to sew **Top**, **Bottom**, then **Side Border Units** to center section to complete **Quilt Top**.

COMPLETING THE QUILT

1. Follow **Quilting**, page 151, to mark, layer, and quilt using **Quilting Diagram** as a suggestion. Our quilt is hand quilted.
2. Cut a 30" square of binding fabric. Follow **Binding**, page 155, to bind quilt using 2¹⁄₂"w bias binding with mitered corners.

Quilting Diagram

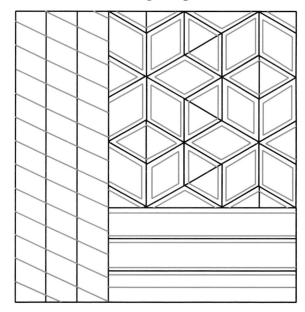

123

LIBERTY
WALL
QUILTS

Add a handmade touch of Americana to your decor with one of our delightful quilted wall hangings. Whether you're creating a hint of country charm or a bit of stately elegance, these scaled-down accents are big on decorative flair. Not only are they made using the best of our time-saving tips, but their smaller size means you can complete them in a jiffy! A great project for novice quilters, our Nine-Patch wall hanging is extra quick because the pieced blocks and the border are created using easy strip sets. Assembled in rows and edged with a contrasting binding, the design is completed with a simple star pattern and in-the-ditch quilting.

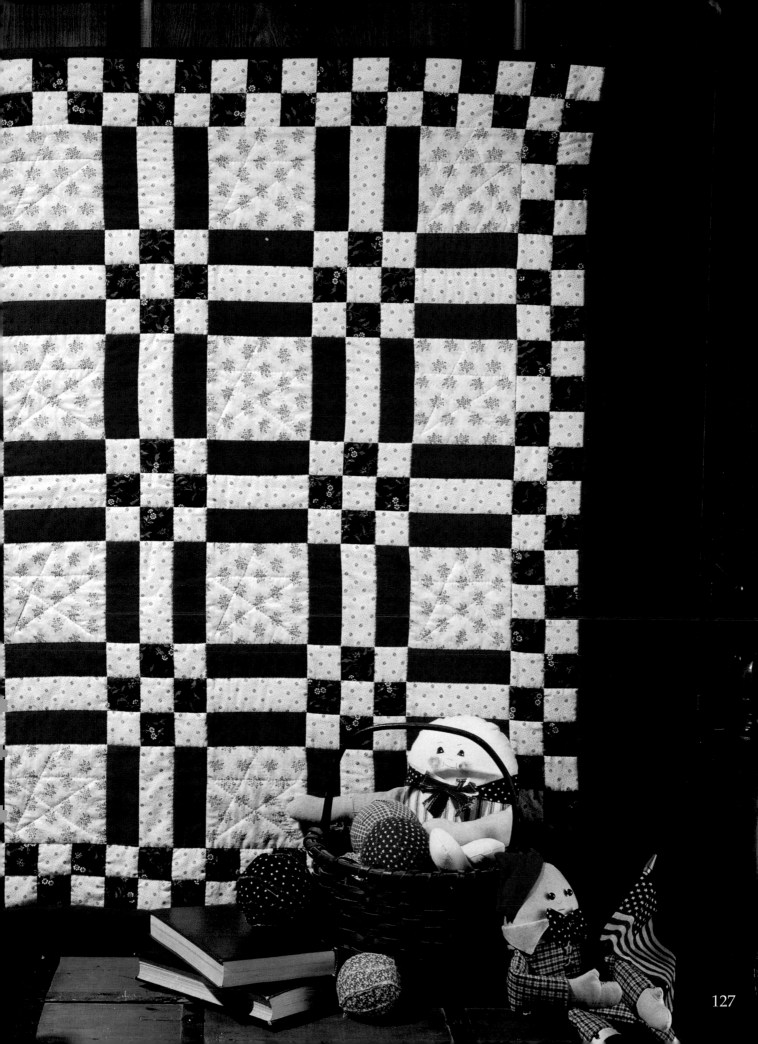

*I*nspired by our Centennial Medallion Collection, this diminutive eagle wall hanging (opposite) re-creates the majestic mood of the dramatic quilt with simpler — and faster — details. The central emblem is fused in place and then machine stitched around the edges using clear nylon thread for a no-fuss finish. Its striped border is accented by corner stars, each created using grid-pieced triangle-squares. The homestyle patchwork of this charming wall hanging (below) earns it a four-star rating for style and ease! Enhanced by an appealing Irish Chain design, the four old-fashioned stars are created using a "sew and flip" technique for precise points.

FOUR-STAR WALL HANGING

SKILL LEVEL: 1 2 3 4 5
WALL HANGING SIZE: 25" x 25"

YARDAGE REQUIREMENTS

Yardage is based on 45"w fabric.

- ☐ ⁵/₈ yd of cream print
- ■ ¼ yd of blue print
- ■ ¼ yd of red print
- ▨ ¼ yd of white stripe
- ▦ ⅛ yd of cream stripe
- ▨ ⅛ yd of gold print
  ⅞ yd for backing and hanging sleeve
  ⅜ yd for binding
  28" x 28" batting

CUTTING OUT THE PIECES

All measurements include a ¼" seam allowance. Follow Rotary Cutting, page 144, to cut fabric. Label cut pieces for easy identification.

1. **From cream print:** ☐
   - Cut 3 strips 3½"w. From these strips, cut 8 **large rectangles** 3½" x 6½", 4 **large squares** 3½" x 3½", and 16 **small rectangles** 3½" x 2".
   - Cut 1 strip 2"w. From this strip, cut 16 **medium squares** 2" x 2".
   - Cut 3 strips 1¼"w. From these strips, cut 24 **rectangle B's** 1¼" x 3½" and 16 **rectangle D's** 1¼" x 2".

2. **From blue print:** ■
   - Cut 3 strips 1¼"w. From these strips, cut 96 **small squares** 1¼" x 1¼".
   - Cut 1 strip 2"w. From this strip, cut 16 **medium squares** 2" x 2".

3. **From red print:** ■
   - Cut 2 strips 2"w. From these strips, cut 32 **medium squares** 2" x 2".

4. **From white stripe:** ▨
   - Cut 5 strips 1¼"w. From these strips, cut 24 **rectangle C's** 1¼" x 5" and 16 **rectangle E's** 1¼" x 2¾".

5. **From cream stripe:** ▦
   - Cut 2 strips 1¼"w. From these strips, cut 24 **rectangle A's** 1¼" x 2" and 16 **small squares** 1¼" x 1¼".

6. **From gold print:** ▨
   - Cut 1 strip 2"w. From this strip, cut 5 **medium squares** 2" x 2" and 4 **rectangle A's** 1¼" x 2".
   - Cut 4 **small squares** 1¼" x 1¼".

ASSEMBLING THE WALL HANGING TOP

Refer to Wall Hanging Top Diagram, page 133, and follow Piecing and Pressing, page 146, to make wall hanging top.

1. Place 1 **medium square** on 1 **small rectangle** and stitch diagonally (**Fig. 1a**). Trim ¼" from stitching line (**Fig. 1b**). Press open, pressing seam allowance toward darker fabric.

Fig. 1a 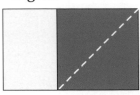 **Fig. 1b**

2. Place 1 **medium square** on opposite end of **small rectangle** and stitch diagonally (**Fig. 2a**). Trim ¼" from stitching line (**Fig. 2b**). Press open, pressing seam allowance toward darker fabric to make **Unit 1**.

Fig. 2a  **Fig. 2b**

Unit 1

3. Repeat Steps 1 and 2 to make a total of 16 **Unit 1's**.
4. Place 1 **medium square** on 1 **large square** and stitch diagonally (**Fig. 3a**). Trim ¼" from stitching line (**Fig. 3b**). Press open, pressing seam allowance toward darker fabric.

Fig. 3a 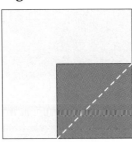 **Fig. 3b**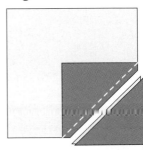

5. Repeat Step 4 to add 1 **medium square** to each remaining corner of **large square** to make **Unit 2**. Make 4 **Unit 2's**.

Unit 2 (make 4)

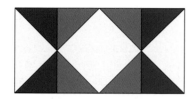

6. Sew 2 **Unit 1's** and 1 **Unit 2** together to make **Unit 3**. Make 4 **Unit 3's**.

Unit 3 (make 4)

7. Sew 2 **medium squares** and 1 **Unit 1** together to make **Unit 4**. Make 8 **Unit 4's**.

Unit 4 (make 8)

8. Sew 1 **Unit 3** and 2 **Unit 4's** together to make **Block A**. Make 4 **Block A's**.

Block A (make 4)

9. Sew 1 **medium square** and 2 **rectangle A's** together to make **Unit 5**. Make 5 **Unit 5's**. Sew 2 **small squares** and 1 **rectangle A** together to make **Unit 6**. Make 14 **Unit 6's**.

Unit 5 (make 5)   **Unit 6** (make 14)

10. Sew 1 **Unit 5** and 2 **Unit 6's** together to make **Unit 7**. Make 5 **Unit 7's**. (Remaining **Unit 6's** will be used in Step 15.)

Unit 7 (make 5)

11. Sew 1 **Unit 7** and 2 **rectangle B's** together to make **Unit 8**. Make 5 **Unit 8's**. Sew 2 **small squares** and 1 **rectangle B** together to make **Unit 9**. Make 14 **Unit 9's**.

Unit 8 (make 5)   **Unit 9** (make 14)

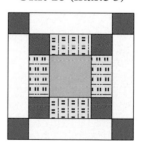   

12. Sew 1 **Unit 8** and 2 **Unit 9's** together to make **Unit 10**. Make 5 **Unit 10's**. (Remaining **Unit 9's** will be used in Step 16.)

Unit 10 (make 5)

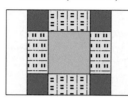

13. Sew 1 **Unit 10** and 2 **rectangle C's** together to make **Unit 11**. Make 5 **Unit 11's**. Sew 2 **small squares** and 1 **rectangle C** together to make **Unit 12**. Make 14 **Unit 12's**.

Unit 11 (make 5)

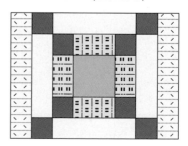

Unit 12 (make 14)

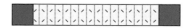

14. Sew 1 **Unit 11** and 2 **Unit 12's** together to make **Block B**. Make 5 **Block B's**. (Remaining **Unit 12's** will be used in Step 17.)

Block B (make 5)

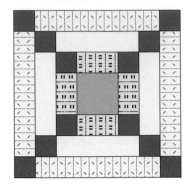

15. Sew 2 **small squares** and 1 **rectangle A** together to make **Unit 13**. Make 4 **Unit 13's**. Sew 1 **Unit 6** and 1 **Unit 13** together to make **Unit 14**. Make 4 **Unit 14's**.

Unit 13 (make 4)   **Unit 14** (make 4)

16. Sew 2 **rectangle D's** and 1 **Unit 14** together to make **Unit 15**. Make 4 **Unit 15's**. Sew 1 **Unit 9** and 1 **Unit 15** together to make **Unit 16**. Make 4 **Unit 16's**.

Unit 15 (make 4)

Unit 16 (make 4)

17. Sew 2 **rectangle E's** and 1 **Unit 16** together to make **Unit 17**. Make 4 **Unit 17's**. Sew 1 **Unit 12** and 1 **Unit 17** together to make **Block C**. Make 4 **Block C's**.

Unit 17 (make 4)

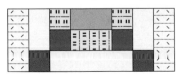

Block C (make 4)

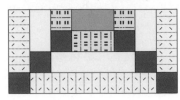

18. Sew 4 **small squares** together to make **Unit 18**. Make 4 **Unit 18's**.

Unit 18 (make 4)

19. Sew 1 **Unit 18** and 1 **rectangle D** together to make **Unit 19**. Make 4 **Unit 19's**.

Unit 19 (make 4)

20. Sew 1 **rectangle D**, 1 **small square**, and 1 **Unit 19** together to make **Unit 20**. Make 4 **Unit 20's**.

Unit 20 (make 4)

21. Sew 2 **rectangle E's**, 1 **small square**, and 1 **Unit 20** together to make **Block D**. Make 4 **Block D's**.

Block D (make 4)

22. Sew 2 **Block D's**, 2 **large rectangles**, and 1 **Block C** together to make **Row A**. Make 2 **Row A's**.

Row A (make 2)

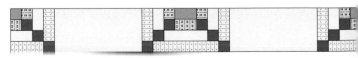

23. Sew 2 **large rectangles**, 2 **Block B's**, and 1 **Block A** together to make **Row B**. Make 2 **Row B's**.

Row B (make 2)

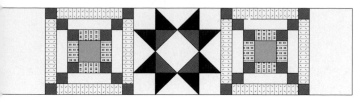

24. Sew 2 **Block C's**, 2 **Block A's**, and 1 **Block B** together to make 1 **Row C**.

Row C (make 1)

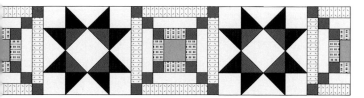

25. Referring to **Wall Hanging Top Diagram**, sew **Rows** together to complete **Wall Hanging Top**.

COMPLETING THE WALL HANGING

1. Follow **Quilting**, page 151, to mark, layer, and quilt using **Quilting Diagram** as a suggestion. Our wall hanging is hand quilted.
2. Follow **Making a Hanging Sleeve**, page 157, to attach hanging sleeve.
3. Follow **Binding**, page 155, to bind wall hanging using 2¹/₂"w straight-grain binding with overlapped corners.

Quilting Diagram

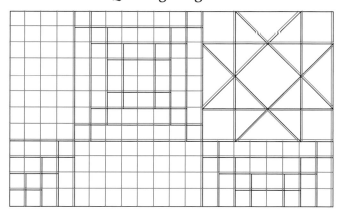

Wall Hanging Top Diagram

EAGLE WALL HANGING

SKILL LEVEL: 1 2 3 4 5
WALL HANGING SIZE: 20" x 32"

YARDAGE REQUIREMENTS

Yardage is based on 45"w fabric.

☐ 1¹/₈ yds of white print
■ ³/₈ yd of blue print
■ ³/₈ yd of red print
▷▷ ¹/₄ yd of white stripe
◪ scraps of red, gold, blue, and brown prints for appliqués
³/₄ yd for backing and hanging sleeve
³/₈ yd for binding
23" x 35" batting

CUTTING OUT THE PIECES

All measurements include a ¹/₄" seam allowance. Follow Rotary Cutting, page 144, to cut fabric.

1. **From white print:** ☐
    *   Cut 4 **top/bottom border strips** 1¹/₂" x 23¹/₄".
    *   Cut 4 **side border strips** 1¹/₂" x 11¹/₂".
    *   Cut 1 **background** 11¹/₂" x 23¹/₄".
    *   From remaining fabric width, cut 1 **large square** 9" x 9" for triangle-squares and 16 **small squares** 1¹/₂" x 1¹/₂".

2. **From blue print:** ■
    *   Cut 1 **large square** 9" x 9" for triangle-squares.
    *   Cut 4 **medium squares** 2¹/₂" x 2¹/₂".

3. **From red print:** ■
    *   Cut 4 **top/bottom border strips** 1" x 23¹/₄".
    *   Cut 4 **side border strips** 1" x 11¹/₂".

4. **From white stripe:** ▷▷
    *   Cut 2 **top/bottom border strips** 1¹/₂" x 23¹/₄".
    *   Cut 2 **side border strips** 1¹/₂" x 11¹/₂".

PREPARING THE APPLIQUÉS

Referring to photo, use patterns, pages 117 - 119, and follow Preparing Fusible Appliqués, page 149, to cut the following pieces from scraps:

> 2 **wings** (1 in reverse)
> 1 **head**
> 1 **tail**
> 1 **shield**
> 1 **shield top**
> 1 **star**
> 2 **arrow shafts**
> 2 **arrowheads**

ASSEMBLING THE WALL HANGING TOP

*Refer to **Wall Hanging Top Diagram** and follow **Piecing and Pressing**, page 146, to make wall hanging top.*

1. Referring to photo, follow **Invisible Appliqué**, page 149, to stitch appliqués to **background**.
2. Sew **side border strips** together to make 2 **Side Border Units**. Using **top/bottom border strips**, repeat to make 2 **Top/Bottom Border Units**.

Border Unit

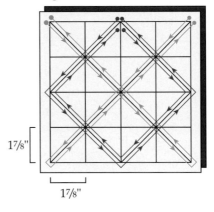

3. To make triangle-squares, place 1 white and 1 blue **large square** right sides together. Referring to **Fig. 1**, follow **Making Triangle-Squares**, page 147, to make 32 **triangle-squares**.

Fig. 1   **triangle-square**
                            (make 32)

1⁷/₈"

1⁷/₈"

4. Reversing colors, follow Steps 2 - 5 of **Making Star Unit** for **Stars & Stripes Quilt**, page 56, to make 4 **Star Units**.
5. Sew **Top** and **Bottom Border Units** to top and bottom edges of **background**. Sew 1 **Star Unit** to each end of each **Side Border Unit**; sew **Side Border Units** to side edges of **background** to complete **Wall Hanging Top**.

COMPLETING THE WALL HANGING

1. Follow **Quilting**, page 151, to mark, layer, and quilt using **Quilting Diagram** as a suggestion. Our wall hanging is hand quilted.
2. Follow **Making a Hanging Sleeve**, page 157, to attach hanging sleeve.
3. Follow **Binding**, page 155, to bind wall hanging using 2¹/₂"w straight-grain binding with overlapped corners.

Wall Hanging Top Diagram

Quilting Diagram

NINE-PATCH WALL HANGING

SKILL LEVEL: 1 2 3 4 5
WALL HANGING SIZE: 39" x 39"

YARDAGE REQUIREMENTS

Yardage is based on 45"w fabric.

☐ ³/₄ yd of white print
▨ ⁵/₈ yd of blue print
■ ¹/₂ yd of red print
✴ ³/₈ yd for white print for squares
1¹/₂ yds for backing and hanging sleeve
³/₄ yd for binding
41" x 41" batting

CUTTING OUT THE PIECES

All measurements include a ¹/₄" seam allowance. Follow
Rotary Cutting, page 144, to cut fabric.

1. **From white print:** ☐
    • Cut 11 **strips** 2"w.

2. **From blue print:** ▨
    • Cut 8 **strips** 2"w.

3. **From red print:** ■
    • Cut 6 **strips** 2"w.

4. **From white print for squares:** ✴
    • Cut 2 strips 5"w. From these strips, cut
      16 **squares** 5" x 5".

ASSEMBLING THE WALL HANGING TOP

*Follow **Piecing and Pressing**, page 146, to make wall hanging top.*

1. Sew 3 **strips** together to make 1 **Strip Set A**. Cut across **Strip Set A** at 2" intervals to make 18 **Unit 1's**.

Strip Set A (make 1)   **Unit 1** (make 18)

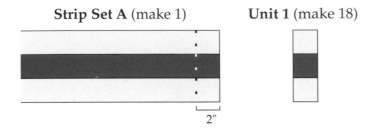

2. Sew 3 **strips** together to make 1 **Strip Set B**. Cut across **Strip Set B** at 2" intervals to make 9 **Unit 2's**.

Strip Set B (make 1)   **Unit 2** (make 9)

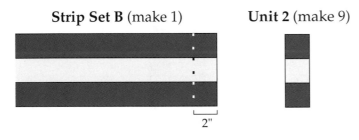

3. Sew 2 **Unit 1's** and 1 **Unit 2** together to make **Unit 3**. Make 9 **Unit 3's**.

Unit 3 (make 9)

4. Sew 3 **strips** together to make **Strip Set C**. Make 3 **Strip Set C's**. Cut across **Strip Set C's** at 5" intervals to make 24 **Unit 4's**.

Strip Set C (make 3)   **Unit 4** (make 24)

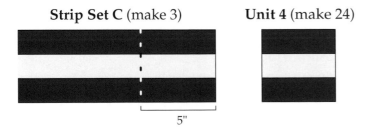

5. Sew 4 **squares** and 3 **Unit 4's** together to make **Row A**. Make 4 **Row A's**.

Row A (make 4)

6. Sew 4 **Unit 4's** and 3 **Unit 3's** together to make **Row B**. Make 3 **Row B's**.

Row B (make 3)

7. Referring to **Wall Hanging Top Diagram**, sew **Rows** together to make center section of wall hanging top.

8. Sew 2 **strips** together to make **Strip Set D**. Make 5 **Strip Set D's**. Cut across **Strip Set D's** at 2" intervals to make 92 **Unit 5's**.

Strip Set D (make 5)   **Unit 5** (make 92)

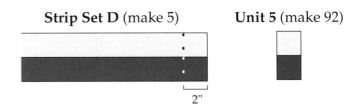

9. Referring to **Wall Hanging Top Diagram**, sew 21 **Unit 5's** together to make **Top/Bottom Border**. Make 2 **Top/Bottom Borders**. Sew 25 **Unit 5's** together to make **Side Border**. Make 2 **Side Borders**.

10. Sew **Top**, **Bottom**, then **Side Borders** to center section to complete **Wall Hanging Top**.

COMPLETING THE WALL HANGING

1. Follow **Quilting**, page 151, to mark, layer, and quilt using **Quilting Diagram** as a suggestion. Our wall hanging is hand quilted.

2. Follow **Making a Hanging Sleeve**, page 157, to attach hanging sleeve.

3. Cut a 22" square of binding fabric. Follow **Binding**, page 155, to bind wall hanging using 2½"w bias binding with mitered corners.

Wall Hanging Top Diagram

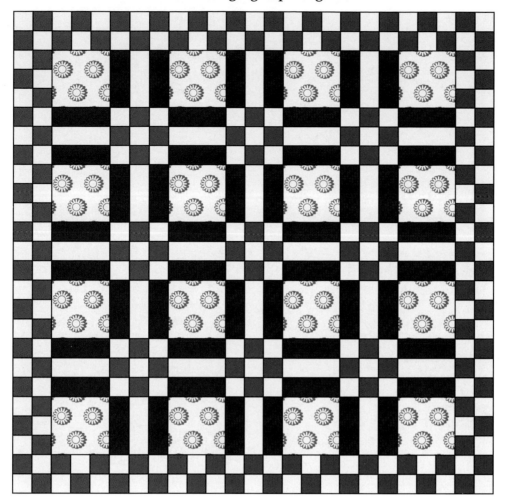

Quilting Diagram

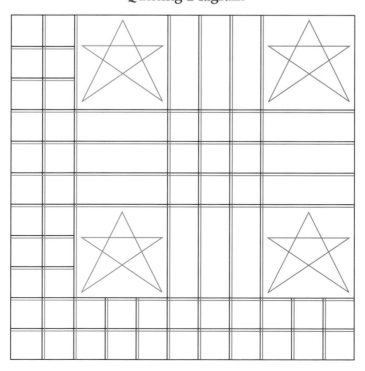

OHIO CHAIN

The Variable Star pattern became a mainstay in American piecework as settlers migrated across the frontier during the early days of Western expansion. Pioneer quilters often honored their new homesteads by renaming the pattern with such titles as Lone Star and Ohio Star. A legacy from the Buckeye State, our Ohio Chain quilt was created with an array of Ohio Star blocks set together without sashing. The result is a dazzling illusion of geometric "chains" suspended on a background of white. Accurate star points are easy to make by cutting and re-assembling triangle-squares — a clever update of traditional piecing! Edged with a blue print inner border and a wider white border, the quilt top is framed in simplicity.

OHIO CHAIN QUILT

SKILL LEVEL: 1 2 3 4 5
BLOCK SIZE: 9" x 9"
QUILT SIZE: 89" x 107"

YARDAGE REQUIREMENTS

Yardage is based on 45"w fabric.

- 8¼ yds of cream solid
- 3 yds of navy print for inner borders
- 1 fat quarter (18" x 22" piece) *each* of 10 navy prints and 10 red prints
  8⅛ yds for backing
  1 yd for binding
  120" x 120" batting

CUTTING OUT THE PIECES

All measurements include a ¼" seam allowance. Follow **Rotary Cutting**, *page 144, to cut fabric.*

1. **From cream solid:** ☐
   - Cut 27 strips 3½"w. From these strips, cut 320 **squares** 3½" x 3½".
   - Cut 2 lengthwise **side outer borders** 6½" x 110".
   - Cut 2 lengthwise **top/bottom outer borders** 6½" x 80".
   - From remaining fabric width, cut 20 **rectangles** 10" x 19" for triangle-squares.

2. **From navy print for inner borders:** ■
   - Cut 2 lengthwise **side inner borders** 2½" x 98".
   - Cut 2 lengthwise **top/bottom inner borders** 2½" x 76".

3. **From *each* navy print and red print:** ◨
   - Cut 1 **rectangle** 10" x 19" for triangle-squares.
   - Cut 4 **squares** 3½" x 3½".

ASSEMBLING THE QUILT TOP

Follow **Piecing and Pressing**, *page 146, to make quilt top.*

1. To make triangle-squares, place 1 navy and 1 cream **rectangle** right sides together. Referring to **Fig. 1**, follow **Making Triangle-Squares**, page 147, to make 16 **triangle-squares**.

Fig. 1

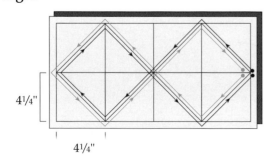

4¼"

4¼"

triangle-square (make 16)

2. Referring to **Fig. 2**, place 2 **triangle-squares** right sides and opposite colors together, matching seams. Referring to **Fig. 3**, draw a diagonal line from corner to corner. Stitch ¼" on both sides of drawn line. Cut apart on drawn line and press open to make 2 **triangle units**. Repeat with remaining triangle-squares to make a total of 16 **triangle units**.

Fig. 2   **Fig. 3**

triangle unit (make 16)

3. Sew 2 cream **squares** and 1 **triangle unit** together to make **Unit 1**. Make 8 **Unit 1's**.

Unit 1 (make 8)

4. Sew 2 **triangle units** and 1 matching navy **square** together to make **Unit 2**. Make 4 **Unit 2's**.

Unit 2 (make 4)

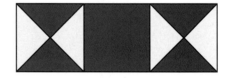

5. Sew 2 **Unit 1's** and 1 **Unit 2** together to make **Block**. Make 4 **Blocks**.

Block (make 4)

5. Using remaining **rectangles** and **squares**, repeat Steps 1 - 5 to make a total of 40 navy **Blocks** and 40 red **Blocks**.
7. Sew 8 **Blocks** together to make **Row**. Make 10 **Rows**.

Row (make 10)

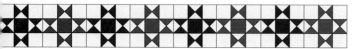

8. Referring to **Quilt Top Diagram**, sew **Rows** together to make center section of quilt top.
9. Follow **Adding Squared Borders**, page 150, to sew **top**, **bottom**, then **side inner borders** to center section. Add **top**, **bottom**, then **side outer borders** to complete **Quilt Top**.

COMPLETING THE QUILT

1. Follow **Quilting**, page 151, to mark, layer, and quilt using **Quilting Diagram** as a suggestion. Our quilt is hand quilted.
2. Cut a 32" square of binding fabric. Follow **Binding**, page 155, to bind quilt using 2¹/₂"w bias binding with mitered corners.

Quilting Diagram

Quilt Top Diagram

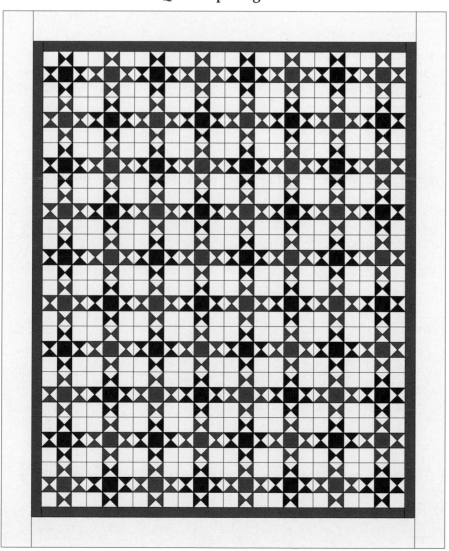

GENERAL INSTRUCTIONS

Complete instructions are given for making each of the quilts and other projects shown in this book. Skill levels indicated for quilts and wall hangings may help you choose the right project. To make your quilting easier and more enjoyable, we encourage you to carefully read all of these general instructions, study the color photographs, and familiarize yourself with the individual project instructions before beginning a project.

QUILTING SUPPLIES

This list includes all the tools you need for basic quick-method quiltmaking, plus additional supplies used for special techniques. Unless otherwise specified, all items may be found in your favorite fabric store or quilt shop.

Batting — Batting is most commonly available in polyester, cotton, or a polyester/cotton blend (see **Choosing and Preparing the Batting**, page 153).

Cutting mat — A cutting mat is a special mat designed to be used with a rotary cutter. A mat that measures approximately 18" x 24" is a good size for most cutting.

Eraser — A soft white fabric eraser or white art eraser may be used to remove pencil marks from fabric. Do not use a colored eraser, as the dye may discolor fabric.

Iron — An iron with both steam and dry settings and a smooth, clean soleplate is necessary for proper pressing.

Marking tools — There are many different types of marking tools available (see **Marking Quilting Lines**, page 152). A silver quilter's pencil is a good marker for both light and dark fabrics.

Masking tape — Two widths of masking tape, 1"w and 1/4"w, are helpful to have when quilting. The 1"w tape is used to secure the backing fabric to a flat surface when layering the quilt. The 1/4"w tape may be used as a guide when outline quilting.

Needles — Two types of needles are used for hand sewing: *Betweens*, used for quilting, are short and strong for stitching through layered fabric and batting. *Sharps* are longer, thinner needles used for basting and other hand sewing. For *sewing machine needles*, we recommend size 10 to 14 or 70 to 90 universal (sharp-pointed) needles.

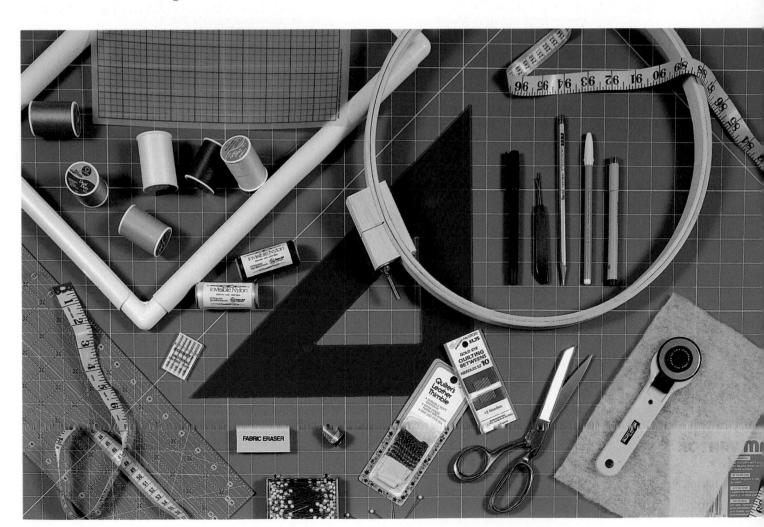

Paper-backed fusible web — This iron-on adhesive with paper backing is used to secure fabric cutouts to another fabric when appliquéing. If the cutouts will be stitched in place, purchase the lighter weight web that will not gum up your sewing machine. A heavier weight web is used for appliqués that are fused in place with no stitching.

Permanent fine-point marker — A permanent marker is used to mark templates and stencils and to sign and date quilts. Test marker on fabric to make sure it will not bleed or wash out.

Pins — Straight pins made especially for quilting are extra long with large, round heads. Glass head pins will stand up to occasional contact with a hot iron. Some quilters prefer extra-fine dressmaker's silk pins. If you are machine quilting, you will need a large supply of 1" long (size 01) rust-proof safety pins for pin-basting.

Quilting hoop or frame — Quilting hoops and frames are designed to securely hold the 3 layers of a quilt together while you quilt. Many different types and sizes are available, including round and oval wooden hoops, frames made of rigid plastic pipe, and large floor frames made of either material. A 14" or 16" hoop allows you to quilt in your lap and makes your quilting portable.

Rotary cutter — The rotary cutter is the essential tool for quick-method quilting techniques. The cutter consists of a round, sharp blade mounted on a handle with a retractable blade guard for safety. It should be used only with a cutting mat and rotary cutting ruler. Two sizes are generally available; we recommend the larger (45 mm) size.

Rotary cutting rulers — A rotary cutting ruler is a thick, clear acrylic ruler made specifically for use with a rotary cutter. It should have accurate 1/8" crosswise and lengthwise markings and markings for 45° and 60° angles. A 6" x 24" ruler is a good size for most cutting. An additional 6" x 12" ruler or 12 1/2" square ruler is helpful when cutting wider pieces. Many specialty rulers are available that make specific cutting tasks faster and easier.

Scissors — Although most cutting will be done with a rotary cutter, sharp, high-quality scissors are still needed for some cutting. A separate pair of scissors for cutting paper and plastic is recommended. Smaller scissors are handy for clipping threads.

Seam ripper — A good seam ripper with a fine point is useful for removing stitching.

Sewing machine — A sewing machine that produces a good, even straight stitch is all that is necessary for most quilting. Zigzag stitch capability is necessary for Invisible Appliqué. Blindstitch with variable stitch width capability is required for Mock Hand Appliqué. Clean and oil your machine often and keep the tension set properly.

Stabilizer — Commercially made non-woven material or paper stabilizer is placed behind background fabric when doing Invisible Appliqué to provide a more stable stitching surface.

Tape measure — A flexible 120" long tape measure is helpful for measuring a quilt top before adding borders.

Template material — Sheets of translucent plastic, often pre-marked with a grid, are made especially for making templates and quilting stencils.

Thimble — A thimble is necessary when hand quilting. Thimbles are available in metal, plastic, or leather and in many sizes and styles. Choose a thimble that fits well and is comfortable.

Thread — Several types of thread are used for quiltmaking: *General-purpose* sewing thread is used for basting, piecing, and some appliquéing. Buy high-quality cotton or cotton-covered polyester thread in light and dark neutrals, such as ecru and grey, for your basic supplies. *Quilting* thread is stronger than general-purpose sewing thread, and some brands have a coating to make them slide more easily through the quilt layers. Some machine appliqué projects in this book use *transparent monofilament* (clear nylon) thread. Use a very fine (.004 mm), soft nylon thread that is not stiff or wiry. Choose clear nylon thread for white or light fabrics or smoke nylon thread for darker fabrics.

Triangle — A large plastic right-angle triangle (available in art and office supply stores) is useful in rotary cutting for making first cuts to "square up" raw edges of fabric and for checking to see that cuts remain at right angles to the fold.

Walking foot — A walking foot or even-feed foot is needed for straight-line machine quilting. This special foot will help all 3 layers of the quilt move at the same rate over the feed dogs to provide a smoother quilted project.

FABRICS
SELECTING FABRICS
For many quilters, choosing fabrics for a new quilt project is one of the most fun, yet most challenging, parts of quiltmaking. Photographs of our quilts are excellent guides for choosing the colors for your quilt. You may choose to duplicate the colors in the photograph, or you may use the same light, medium, and dark values in completely different color families. When you change the light and dark value placement in a quilt block, you may come up with a surprising new creation. The most important lesson to learn about fabrics and color is to choose fabrics you love. When you combine several fabrics you are simply crazy about in a quilt, you are sure to be happy with the results!

The yardage requirements listed for each project are based on 45" wide fabric with a "usable" width of 42" after shrinkage and trimming selvages. Your actual usable width will probably vary slightly from fabric to fabric. Though most fabrics will yield 42" or more, if you find a fabric that you suspect will yield a narrower usable width you will need to purchase additional yardage to compensate. Our recommended yardage lengths should be adequate for occasional resquaring of fabric when many cuts are required, but it never hurts to buy a little more fabric for insurance against a narrower usable width, the occasional cutting error, or to have on hand for making coordinating projects.

Choose high-quality, medium-weight, 100% cotton fabrics such as broadcloth or calico. All-cotton fabrics hold a crease better, fray less, and are easier to quilt than cotton/polyester blends. All the fabrics for a quilt should be of comparable weight and weave. Check the end of the fabric bolt for fiber content and width.

PREPARING FABRICS
All fabrics should be washed, dried, and pressed before cutting.

1. To check colorfastness before washing, cut a small piece of the fabric and place in a glass of hot water with a little detergent. Leave fabric in the water for a few minutes. Remove from water and blot fabric with white paper towels. If any color bleeds onto the towels, wash the fabric separately with warm water and detergent, then rinse until the water runs clear. If fabric continues to bleed, choose another fabric.
2. Unfold yardage and separate fabrics by color. To help reduce raveling, use scissors to snip a small triangle from each corner of your fabric pieces. Machine wash fabrics in warm water with a small amount of mild laundry detergent. Do not use fabric softener. Rinse well and then dry fabrics in the dryer, checking long fabric lengths occasionally to make sure they are not tangling.
3. To make ironing easier, remove fabrics from dryer while they are slightly damp. Refold each fabric lengthwise (as it was on the bolt) with wrong sides together and matching selvages. If necessary, adjust slightly at selvages so that fold lies flat. Press each fabric with a steam iron set on "Cotton."

ROTARY CUTTING

*Based on the idea that you can easily cut strips of fabric and then cut those strips into smaller pieces, rotary cutting has brought speed and accuracy to quiltmaking. Observe safety precautions when using the rotary cutter since it is extremely sharp. Develop a habit of retracting the blade guard **just before** making a cut and closing it **immediately afterward**, before laying down the cutter.*

1. Follow **Preparing Fabrics** to wash, dry, and press fabrics.
2. Cut all strips from the selvage-to-selvage width of the fabric unless otherwise indicated. Place fabric on the cutting mat as shown in **Fig. 1** with the fold of the fabric toward you. To straighten the uneven fabric edge, make the first "squaring up" cut by placing the right edge of the rotary cutting ruler over the left raw edge of the fabric. Place right-angle triangle (or another rotary cutting ruler) with the lower edge carefully aligned with the fold and the left edge against the ruler (**Fig. 1**). Hold the ruler firmly with your left hand, placing your little finger off the left edge to anchor the ruler. Remove the triangle, pick up the rotary cutter, and retract the blade guard. Using a smooth, downward motion, make the cut by running the blade of the rotary cutter firmly along the right edge of the ruler (**Fig. 2**). **Always** cut in a direction **away** from your body and **immediately** close the blade guard after each cut.

Fig. 1

Fig. 2

3. To cut each of the strips required for the project, place the ruler over the cut edge of the fabric, aligning desired marking on the ruler with the cut edge (**Fig. 3**) and then make the cut. When cutting several strips from a single piece of fabric, it is important to occasionally use the ruler and triangle to ensure that cuts are still at a perfect right angle to the fold. If not, repeat Step 2 to straighten.

Fig. 3

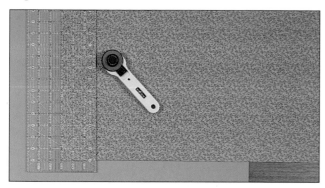

4. To square up selvage ends of a strip before cutting pieces, refer to **Fig. 4** and place folded strip on mat with selvage ends to your right. Aligning a horizontal marking on ruler with 1 long edge of strip, use rotary cutter to trim off selvage to make end of strip square and even (**Fig. 4**). Turn strip (or entire mat) so that cut end is to your left before making subsequent cuts.

Fig. 4

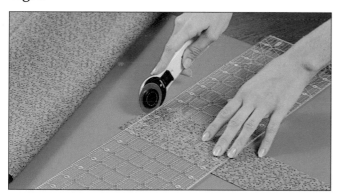

5. Pieces such as rectangles and squares can now be cut from strips. (Cutting other shapes such as diamonds is discussed in individual project instructions.) Usually strips remain folded, and pieces are cut in pairs after ends of strips are squared up. To cut squares or rectangles from a strip, place ruler over left end of strip, aligning desired marking on ruler with cut end of strip. To ensure perfectly square cuts, align a horizontal marking on ruler with 1 long edge of strip (**Fig. 5**) before making the cut.

Fig. 5

6. To cut 2 triangles from a square, cut square the size indicated in the project instructions. Cut square once diagonally to make 2 triangles (**Fig. 6**).

Fig. 6

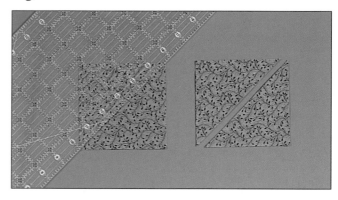

7. To cut 4 triangles from a square, cut square the size indicated in the project instructions. Cut square twice diagonally to make 4 triangles (**Fig. 7**). You may find it helpful to use a small rotary cutting mat so that mat can be turned to make second cut without disturbing fabric pieces.

Fig. 7

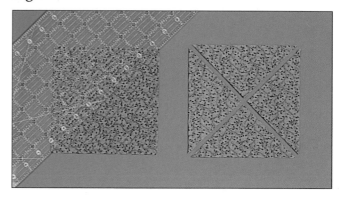

8. After some practice, you may want to try stacking up to 6 fabric layers when making cuts. When stacking strips, match long cut edges and follow Step 4 to square up ends of strip stack. Carefully turn stack (or entire mat) so that squared-up ends are to your left before making subsequent cuts. After cutting, check accuracy of pieces. Some shapes, such as diamonds, are more difficult to cut accurately in stacks.

9. In some cases, strips will be sewn together into strip sets before being cut into smaller units. When cutting a strip set, align a seam in strip set with a horizontal marking on the ruler to maintain square cuts (**Fig. 8**). We do not recommend stacking strip sets for rotary cutting.

Fig. 8

10. Most borders for quilts in this book are cut along the more stable lengthwise grain to minimize wavy edges caused by stretching. To remove selvages before cutting lengthwise strips, place fabric on mat with selvages to your left and squared-up end at bottom of mat. Placing ruler over selvage and using squared-up edge instead of fold, follow Step 2 to cut away selvages as you did raw edges (**Fig. 9**). After making a cut the length of the mat, move the next section of fabric to be cut onto the mat. Repeat until you have removed selvages from required length of fabric.

Fig. 9

11. After removing selvages, place ruler over left edge of fabric, aligning desired marking on ruler with cut edge of fabric. Make cuts as in Step 3. After each cut, move next section of fabric onto mat as in Step 10.

PIECING AND PRESSING

Precise cutting, followed by accurate piecing and careful pressing, will ensure that all the pieces of your quilt top fit together well.

PIECING

Set sewing machine stitch length for approximately 11 stitches per inch. Use a new, sharp needle suited for medium-weight woven fabric.

Use a neutral-colored general-purpose sewing thread (not quilting thread) in the needle and in the bobbin. Stitch first on a scrap of fabric to check upper and bobbin thread tension; make any adjustments necessary.

For good results, it is **essential** that you stitch with an **accurate ¼" seam allowance**. On many sewing machines, the measurement from the needle to the outer edge of the presser foot is ¼". If this is the case with your machine, the presser foot is your best guide. If not, measure ¼" from the needle and mark with a piece of masking tape. Special presser feet that are exactly ¼" wide are also available for most sewing machines.

When piecing, **always** place pieces **right sides together** and **match raw edges**; pin if necessary. (If using straight pins, remove the pins just before they reach the sewing machine needle.)

Chain Piecing

Chain piecing whenever possible will make your work go faster and will usually result in more accurate piecing. Stack the pieces you will be sewing beside your machine in the order you will need them and in a position that will allow you to easily pick them up. Pick up each pair of pieces, carefully place them together as they will be sewn, and feed them into the machine one after the other. Stop between each pair only long enough to pick up the next and don't cut thread between pairs (**Fig. 10**). After all pieces are sewn, cut threads, press, and go on to the next step, chain piecing when possible.

Fig 10

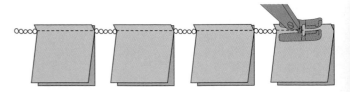

Sewing Strip Sets

When there are several strips to assemble into a strip set, first sew the strips together into pairs, then sew the pairs together to form the strip set. To help avoid distortion, sew 1 seam in 1 direction and then sew the next seam in the opposite direction (**Fig. 11**).

Fig. 11

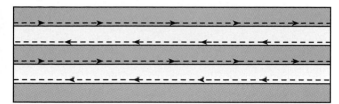

Sewing Across Seam Intersections

When sewing across the intersection of 2 seams, place pieces right sides together and match seams exactly, making sure seam allowances are pressed in opposite directions (**Fig. 12**). To prevent fabric from shifting, you may wish to pin in place.

Fig. 12

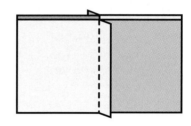

Sewing Sharp Points

To ensure sharp points when joining triangular or diagonal pieces, stitch across the center of the "X" (shown in pink) formed on the wrong side by previous seams (**Fig. 13**).

Fig. 13

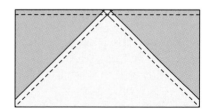

Sewing Bias Seams

Care should be used in handling and stitching bias edges, since they stretch easily. After sewing the seam, carefully press seam allowances to 1 side, making sure not to stretch the fabric.

Making Triangle-Squares

The grid method for making triangle-squares is faster and more accurate than cutting and sewing individual triangles. Stitching before cutting the triangle-squares apart also prevents stretching the bias edges.

1. Follow project instructions to cut rectangles or squares of fabric for making triangle-squares. Place the indicated pieces right sides together and press.
2. On the wrong side of the lighter fabric, draw a grid of squares similar to that shown in **Fig. 14**. The size and number of squares will be given in the project instructions.

Fig. 14

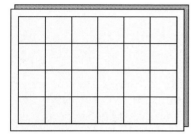

3. Following the example given in the project instructions, draw 1 diagonal line through each square in the grid (**Fig. 15**).

Fig. 15

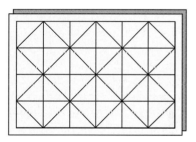

4. Stitch 1/4" on each side of all diagonal lines. For accuracy, it may be helpful to first draw your stitching lines onto the fabric, especially if your presser foot is not your 1/4" guide. In some cases, stitching may be done in a single continuous line. Project instructions include a diagram similar to **Fig. 16**, which shows stitching lines and the direction of the stitching.

Fig. 16

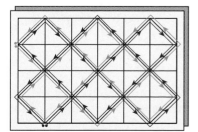

5. Use rotary cutter and ruler to cut along all drawn lines of the grid. Each square of the grid will yield 2 triangle-squares (**Fig. 17**).

Fig. 17

6. Carefully press triangle-squares open, pressing seam allowances toward darker fabric. Trim off points of seam allowances that extend beyond edges of triangle-square (see **Fig. 22**).

Working with Diamonds and Set-in Seams

Piecing diamonds and sewing set-in seams require special handling. For best results, carefully follow the steps below.

1. When sewing 2 diamond pieces together, place pieces right sides together, carefully matching edges; pin. Mark a small dot ¹/₄" from corner of 1 piece as shown in **Fig. 18**. Stitch pieces together in the direction shown, stopping at center of dot and backstitching.

Fig. 18

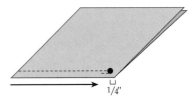

2. For best results, add side triangles, then corner squares to diamond sections. Mark corner of each piece to be set in with a small dot (**Fig. 19**).

Fig. 19

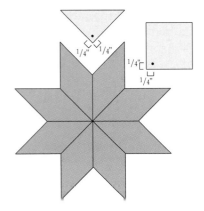

3. To sew first seam, match right sides and pin the triangle or square to the diamond on the left. Stitch seam from the outer edge to the dot, backstitching at the dot; clip threads (**Fig. 20**).

Fig. 20

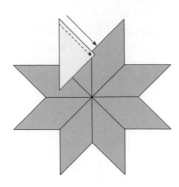

4. To sew the second seam, pivot the added triangle or square to match raw edges of next diamond. Beginning at dot, take 2 or 3 stitches, then backstitch, making sure not to backstitch into previous seam allowance. Continue stitching to outer edge (**Fig. 21**).

Fig. 21

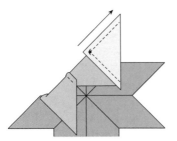

Trimming Seam Allowances

When sewing with diamond or triangle pieces, some seam allowances may extend beyond the edges of the sewn pieces. Trim away "dog ears" that extend beyond the edges of the sewn pieces (**Fig. 22**).

Fig. 22

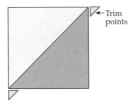

PRESSING

Use a steam iron set on "Cotton" for all pressing. Press as you sew, taking care to prevent small folds along seamlines. Seam allowances are almost always pressed to one side, usually toward the darker fabric. However, to reduce bulk it may occasionally be necessary to press seam allowances toward the lighter fabric or even to press them open. In order to prevent a dark fabric seam allowance from showing through a light fabric, trim the darker seam allowance slightly narrower than the lighter seam allowance. To press long seams, such as those in long strip sets, without curving or other distortion, lay strips across the width of the ironing board.

APPLIQUÉ

PREPARING FUSIBLE APPLIQUÉS

Patterns are printed in reverse to enable you to use our speedy method of preparing appliqués. White or light-colored fabrics may need to be lined with fusible interfacing before applying fusible web to prevent darker fabrics from showing through.

1. Place paper-backed fusible web, web side down, over appliqué pattern. Use a pencil to trace pattern onto paper side of web as many times as indicated in project instructions for a single fabric. Repeat for additional patterns and fabrics.
2. Follow manufacturer's instructions to fuse traced patterns to wrong side of fabrics. Do not remove paper backing.
3. Some projects may have pieces that are given as measurements (such as a 2" x 4" rectangle) instead of drawn patterns. Fuse web to wrong side of the fabrics indicated for these pieces.
4. Use scissors to cut out appliqué pieces along traced lines; use rotary cutting equipment to cut out appliqué pieces given as measurements. Remove paper backing from all pieces.

INVISIBLE APPLIQUÉ

This method of appliqué is an adaptation of satin stitch appliqué that uses clear nylon thread to secure the appliqué pieces. Transparent monofilament (clear nylon) thread is available in 2 colors: clear and smoke. Use clear on white or very light fabrics and smoke on darker colors.

1. Referring to diagram and/or photo, arrange appliqués on the background fabric and follow manufacturer's instructions to fuse in place.
2. Pin a stabilizer, such as paper or any of the commercially available products, on wrong side of background fabric before stitching appliqués in place.
3. Thread sewing machine with transparent monofilament thread; use general-purpose thread that matches background fabric in bobbin.
4. Set sewing machine for a very narrow (approximately $\frac{1}{16}$") zigzag stitch and a short stitch length. You may find that loosening the top tension slightly will yield a smoother stitch.
5. Begin by stitching 2 or 3 stitches in place (drop feed dogs or set stitch length at 0) to anchor thread. Most of the zigzag stitch should be done on the appliqué with the right edges of the stitch falling at the very outside edge of the appliqué. Stitch over all exposed raw edges of appliqué pieces.
6. (*Note:* Dots on **Figs. 23 - 28** indicate where to leave needle in fabric when pivoting.) For **outside corners**, stitch just past the corner, stopping with the needle in **background** fabric (**Fig. 23**). Raise presser foot. Pivot project, lower presser foot, and stitch adjacent side (**Fig. 24**).

Fig. 23   **Fig. 24**

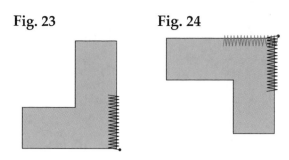

7. For **inside corners**, stitch just past the corner, stopping with the needle in **appliqué** fabric (**Fig. 25**). Raise presser foot. Pivot project, lower presser foot, and stitch adjacent side (**Fig. 26**).

Fig. 25   **Fig. 26**

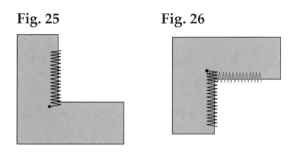

8. When stitching **outside** curves, stop with needle in **background** fabric. Raise presser foot and pivot project as needed. Lower presser foot and continue stitching, pivoting as often as necessary to follow curve (**Fig. 27**).

Fig. 27

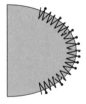

9. When stitching **inside** curves, stop with needle in **appliqué** fabric. Raise presser foot and pivot project as needed. Lower presser foot and continue stitching, pivoting as often as necessary to follow curve (**Fig. 28**).

Fig. 28

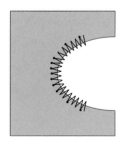

10. Do not backstitch at end of stitching. Pull threads to wrong side of background fabric; knot thread and trim ends.
11. Carefully tear away stabilizer.

MOCK HAND APPLIQUÉ

*This technique uses the blindstitch on your sewing machine to achieve a look that closely resembles traditional hand appliqué. Using an updated method, appliqués are prepared with turned-under edges and then machine stitched to the background fabric. For best appliqué results, your sewing machine must have blindstitch capability with a **variable** stitch width. If your blindstitch width cannot be adjusted, you may still wish to try this technique to see if you are happy with the results. Some sewing machines have a narrower blindstitch width than others.*

1. Follow project instructions to prepare appliqué pieces.
2. Thread needle of sewing machine with transparent monofilament thread; use general-purpose thread in bobbin in a color to match background fabric.
3. Set sewing machine for narrow blindstitch (just wide enough to catch 2 or 3 threads of the appliqué) and a very short stitch length (20 - 30 stitches per inch).
4. Arrange appliqué pieces on background fabric as described in project instructions. Use pins or hand baste to secure.
5. (*Note:* Follow Steps 6 - 9 of **Invisible Appliqué**, page 149, for needle position when pivoting.) Sew around edges of each appliqué so that the straight stitches fall on the background fabric very near the appliqué and the "hem" stitches barely catch the folded edge of the appliqué (**Fig. 29**).

Fig. 29

6. It is not necessary to backstitch at the beginning or end of stitching. End stitching by sewing 1/4" over the first stitches. Trim thread ends close to fabric.
7. To reduce bulk, turn project over and use scissors to cut away background fabric approximately 1/4" inside stitching line of appliqué as shown in **Fig. 30**.

Fig. 30

wrong side

BORDERS

Borders cut along the lengthwise grain will lie flatter than borders cut along the crosswise grain. In most cases, our instructions for cutting borders for bed-size quilts include an extra 2" of length at each end for "insurance"; borders will be trimmed after measuring completed center section of quilt top.

ADDING SQUARED BORDERS

1. Mark the center of each edge of quilt top.
2. Squared borders are usually added to top and bottom, then side edges of the center section of a quilt top. To add top and bottom borders, measure across center of quilt top to determine length of borders (**Fig. 31**). Trim top and bottom borders to the determined length.

Fig. 31

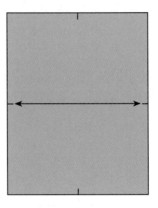

3. Mark center of 1 long edge of top border. Matching center marks and raw edges, pin border to quilt top, easing in any fullness; stitch. Repeat for bottom border.
4. Measure center of quilt top, including attached borders, to determine length of side borders. Trim side borders to the determined length. Repeat Step 3 to add borders to quilt top (**Fig. 32**).

Fig. 32

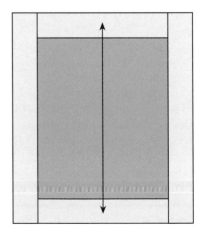

ADDING MITERED BORDERS

1. Mark the center of each edge of quilt top.
2. Mark center of 1 long edge of top border. Measure across center of quilt top (see **Fig. 31**). Matching center marks and raw edges, pin border to center of quilt top edge. Beginning at center of border, measure ½ the width of the quilt top in both directions and mark. Match marks on border with corners of quilt top and pin. Easing in any fullness, pin border to quilt top between center and corners. Sew border to quilt top, beginning and ending seams **exactly** ¼" from each corner of quilt top and backstitching at beginning and end of stitching (**Fig. 33**).

Fig. 33

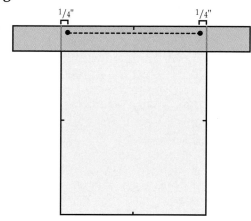

3. Repeat Step 2 to sew bottom, then side borders, to center section of quilt top. To temporarily move first 2 borders out of the way, fold and pin ends as shown in **Fig. 34**.

Fig. 34

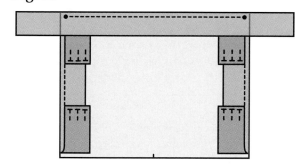

4. Fold 1 corner of quilt top diagonally with right sides together and matching edges. Use ruler to mark stitching line as shown in **Fig. 35**. Pin borders together along drawn line. Sew on drawn line, backstitching at beginning and end of stitching (**Fig. 36**).

Fig. 35

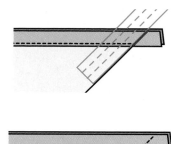

Fig. 36

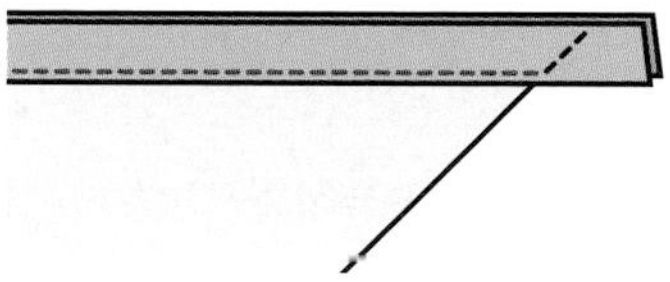

5. Turn mitered corner right side up. Check to make sure corner will lie flat with no gaps or puckers.
6. Trim seam allowance to ¼"; press to 1 side.
7. Repeat Steps 4 - 6 to miter each remaining corner.

QUILTING

Quilting holds the 3 layers (top, batting, and backing) of the quilt together and can be done by hand or machine. Our project instructions tell you which method is used on each project and show you quilting diagrams that can be used as suggestions for marking quilting designs. Because marking, layering, and quilting are interrelated and may be done in different orders depending on circumstances, please read this entire section, pages 151 - 154, before beginning the quilting process on your project.

TYPES OF QUILTING

In the Ditch

Quilting very close to a seamline (**Fig. 37**) or appliqué (**Fig. 38**, page 152) is called "in the ditch" quilting. This type of quilting does not need to be marked and is indicated on our quilting diagrams with blue lines close to seamlines. When quilting in the ditch, quilt on the side **opposite** the seam allowance.

Fig. 37

Fig. 38

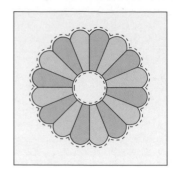

Outline Quilting

Quilting approximately ¼" from a seam or appliqué is called "outline" quilting (**Fig. 39**). This type of quilting is indicated on our quilting diagrams by blue lines a short distance from seamlines. Outline quilting may be marked, or you may place ¼"w masking tape along seamlines and quilt along the opposite edge of the tape. (Do not leave tape on quilt longer than necessary, since it may leave an adhesive residue.)

Fig. 39

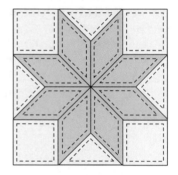

Ornamental Quilting

Quilting decorative lines or designs is called "ornamental" quilting (**Fig. 40**). Ornamental quilting is indicated on our quilting diagrams by blue lines. This type of quilting should be marked before you baste quilt layers together.

Fig. 40

MARKING QUILTING LINES

Fabric marking pencils, various types of chalk markers, and fabric marking pens with inks that disappear with exposure to air or water are readily available and work well for different applications. Lead pencils work well on light-colored fabric, but marks may be difficult to remove. White pencils work well on dark-colored fabric, and silver pencils show up well on many colors. Since chalk rubs off easily, it's a good choice if you are marking as you quilt. Fabric marking pens make more durable and visible markings, but the marks should be carefully removed according to manufacturer's instructions. Press down only as hard as necessary to make a visible line.

When you choose to mark your quilt, whether before or after the layers are basted together, is also a factor in deciding which marking tool to use. If you mark with chalk or a chalk pencil, handling the quilt during basting may rub off the markings. Intricate or ornamental designs may not be practical to mark as you quilt; mark these designs before basting using a more durable marker.

To choose marking tools, take all these factors into consideration and **test** different markers **on scrap fabric** until you find the one that gives the desired result.

USING QUILTING STENCILS

A wide variety of pre-cut quilting stencils, as well as entire books of quilting patterns, are available at your local quilt shop or fabric store. Wherever you draw your quilting inspiration from, using a stencil makes it easier to mark intricate or repetitive designs on your quilt top.

1. To make a stencil from a pattern, center template plastic over pattern and use a permanent marker to trace pattern onto plastic.
2. Use a craft knife with a single or double blade to cut narrow slits along traced lines (**Fig. 41**).

Fig. 41

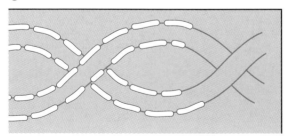

3. Use desired marking tool and stencil to mark quilting lines.

CHOOSING AND PREPARING THE BACKING

To allow for slight shifting of the quilt top during quilting, the backing should be approximately 4" larger on all sides for a bed-size quilt top or approximately 2" larger on all sides for a wall hanging. Yardage requirements listed for quilt backings are calculated for 45"w fabric. If you are making a bed-size quilt, using 90"w or 108"w fabric for the backing may eliminate piecing. To piece a backing using 45"w fabric, use the following instructions.

1. Measure length and width of quilt top; add 8" (4" for a wall hanging) to each measurement.
2. If quilt top is 76"w or less, cut backing fabric into 2 lengths slightly longer than the determined **length** measurement. Trim selvages. Place lengths with right sides facing and sew long edges together, forming a tube (**Fig. 42**). Match seams and press along 1 fold (**Fig. 43**). Cut along pressed fold to form a single piece (**Fig. 44**).

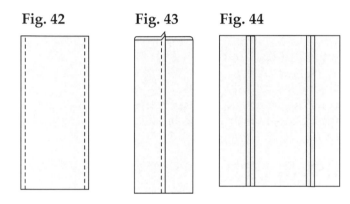

Fig. 42   **Fig. 43**   **Fig. 44**

3. If quilt top is more than 76"w, cut backing fabric into 3 lengths slightly longer than the determined **width** measurement. Trim selvages. Sew long edges together to form a single piece.
4. Trim backing to correct size, if necessary, and press seam allowances open.

CHOOSING AND PREPARING THE BATTING

Choosing the right batting will make your quilting job easier. For fine hand quilting, choose a low-loft batting in any of the fiber types described here. Machine quilters will want to choose a low-loft batting that is all cotton or a cotton/polyester blend because the cotton helps "grip" the layers of the quilt. If the quilt is to be tied, a high-loft batting, sometimes called extra-loft or fat batting, is a good choice.

Batting is available in many different fibers. Bonded polyester batting is one of the most popular batting types. It is treated with a protective coating to stabilize the fibers and to reduce "bearding," a process where batting fibers work their way out through the quilt fabrics. Other batting options include cotton/polyester batting, which combines the best of both polyester and cotton battings; all-cotton batting, which must be quilted more closely than polyester batting; and wool and silk battings, which are generally more expensive and are usually only dry-cleanable.

Whichever batting you choose, read the manufacturer's instructions closely for any special notes on care or preparation. When you're ready to use your chosen batting in a project, cut the batting the same size as the prepared backing.

LAYERING THE QUILT

1. Examine wrong side of quilt top closely; trim any seam allowances and clip any threads that may show through the front of the quilt. Press quilt top.
2. If quilt top is to be marked before layering, mark quilting lines (see **Marking Quilting Lines**, page 152).
3. Place backing **wrong** side up on a flat surface. Use masking tape to tape edges of backing to surface. Place batting on top of backing fabric. Smooth batting gently, being careful not to stretch or tear. Center quilt top **right** side up on batting.
4. If hand quilting, begin in the center and work toward the outer edges to hand baste all layers together. Use long stitches and place basting lines approximately 4" apart (**Fig. 45**). Smooth fullness or wrinkles toward outer edges.

Fig. 45

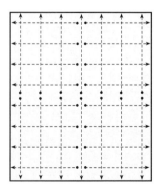

5. If machine quilting, use 1" rust-proof safety pins to "pin-baste" all layers together, spacing pins approximately 4" apart. Begin at the center and work toward the outer edges to secure all layers. If possible, place pins away from areas that will be quilted, although pins may be removed as needed when quilting.

HAND QUILTING

The quilting stitch is a basic running stitch that forms a broken line on the quilt top and backing. Stitches on the quilt top and backing should be straight and equal in length.

1. Secure center of quilt in hoop or frame. Check quilt top and backing to make sure they are smooth. To help prevent puckers, always begin quilting in the center of the quilt and work toward the outside edges.
2. Thread needle with an 18" - 20" length of quilting thread; knot 1 end. Using a thimble, insert needle into quilt top and batting approximately ¹/₂" from where you wish to begin quilting. Bring needle up at the point where you wish to begin (**Fig. 46**); when knot catches on quilt top, give thread a quick, short pull to "pop" knot through fabric into batting (**Fig. 47**).

Fig. 46

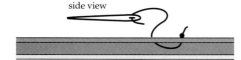

side view

Fig. 47

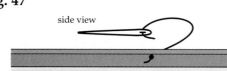

side view

3. Holding the needle with your sewing hand and placing your other hand underneath the quilt, use thimble to push the tip of the needle down through all layers. As soon as needle touches your finger underneath, use that finger to push the tip of the needle only back up through the layers to top of quilt. (The amount of the needle showing above the fabric determines the length of the quilting stitch.) Referring to **Fig. 48**, rock the needle up and down, taking 3 - 6 stitches before bringing the needle and thread completely through the layers. Check the back of the quilt to make sure stitches are going through all layers. When quilting through a seam allowance or quilting a curve or corner, you may need to take 1 stitch at a time.

Fig. 48

4. When you reach the end of your thread, knot thread close to the fabric and "pop" knot into batting; clip thread close to fabric.
5. Stop and move your hoop as often as necessary. You do not have to tie a knot every time you move your hoop; you may leave the thread dangling and pick it up again when you return to that part of the quilt.

MACHINE QUILTING

The machine-quilted project in this book features straight-line quilting, which requires a walking foot or even-feed foot. The term "straight-line" is somewhat deceptive, since curves (especially gentle ones) as well as straight lines can be stitched with this technique.

1. Wind your sewing machine bobbin with general-purpose thread that matches the quilt backing. Do not use quilting thread. Thread the needle of your machine with transparent monofilament thread if you want your quilting to blend with your quilt top fabrics. Use decorative thread, such as a metallic or contrasting-colored general-purpose thread, when you want the quilting lines to stand out more. Set the stitch length for 6 - 10 stitches per inch and attach the walking foot to sewing machine.
2. After pin-basting, decide which section of the quilt will have the longest continuous quilting line, oftentimes the area from center top to center bottom. Leaving the area exposed where you will place your first line of quilting, roll up each edge of the quilt to help reduce the bulk, keeping fabrics smooth. Smaller projects may not need to be rolled.
3. Start stitching at beginning of longest quilting line, using very short stitches for the first ¹/₄" to "lock" beginning of quilting line. Stitch across project, using one hand on each side of the walking foot to slightly spread the fabric and to guide the fabric through the machine. Lock stitches at end of quilting line.
4. Continue machine quilting, stitching the longer quilting lines first to stabilize the quilt before moving on to other areas.

BINDING

Binding encloses the raw edges of your quilt. Because of its stretchiness, bias binding works well for binding projects with curves or rounded corners and tends to lie smooth and flat in any given circumstance. It is also more durable than other types of binding. Binding may also be cut from the straight lengthwise or crosswise grain of the fabric. You will find that straight-grain binding works well for projects with straight edges.

MAKING CONTINUOUS BIAS STRIP BINDING

Bias strips for binding can simply be cut and pieced to the desired length. However, when a long length of binding is needed, the "continuous" method is quick and accurate.

1. Cut a square from binding fabric the size indicated in the project instructions. Cut square in half diagonally to make 2 triangles.
2. With right sides together and using a ¼" seam allowance, sew triangles together (**Fig. 49**); press seam allowance open.

Fig. 49

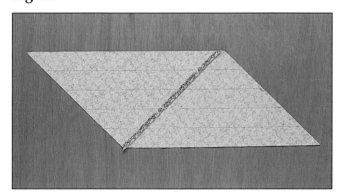

3. On wrong side of fabric, draw lines the width of the binding as specified in the project instructions, usually 2½" (**Fig. 50**). Cut off any remaining fabric less than this width.

Fig. 50

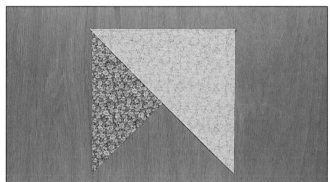

4. With right sides inside, bring short edges together to form a tube; match raw edges so that first drawn line of top section meets second drawn line of bottom section (**Fig. 51**).

Fig. 51

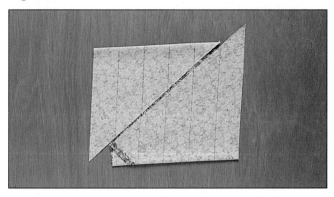

5. Carefully pin edges together by inserting pins through drawn lines at the point where drawn lines intersect, making sure the pins go through intersections on both sides. Using a ¼" seam allowance, sew edges together. Press seam allowance open.
6. To cut continuous strip, begin cutting along first drawn line (**Fig. 52**). Continue cutting along drawn line around tube.

Fig. 52

7. Trim ends of bias strip square.
8. Matching wrong sides and raw edges, press bias strip in half lengthwise to complete binding.

MAKING STRAIGHT-GRAIN BINDING

1. To determine length of strip needed if attaching binding with mitered corners, measure edges of the quilt and add 12".
2. To determine lengths of strips needed if attaching binding with overlapped corners, measure each edge of quilt; add 3" to each measurement.
3. Cut lengthwise or crosswise strips of binding fabric the determined length and the width called for in the project instructions. Strips may be pieced to achieve the necessary length.
4. Matching wrong sides and raw edges, press strip(s) in half lengthwise to complete binding.

ATTACHING BINDING WITH MITERED CORNERS

1. Press 1 end of binding diagonally (**Fig. 53**).

Fig. 53

2. Lay binding around quilt to make sure that seams in binding will not end up at a corner. Adjust placement if necessary. Matching raw edges of binding to raw edge of quilt top and beginning with pressed end several inches from a corner, pin binding to right side of quilt along 1 edge.
3. When you reach the first corner, mark $1/4$" from corner of quilt top (**Fig. 54**).

Fig. 54

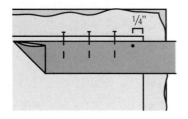

4. Using a $1/4$" seam allowance, sew binding to quilt, backstitching at beginning of stitching and when you reach the mark (**Fig. 55**). Lift needle out of fabric and clip thread.

Fig. 55

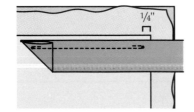

5. Fold binding as shown in **Figs. 56** and **57** and pin binding to adjacent side, matching raw edges. When you reach the next corner, mark $1/4$" from edge of quilt top.

Fig. 56   **Fig. 57**

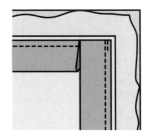

6. Backstitching at edge of quilt top, sew pinned binding to quilt (**Fig. 58**); backstitch when you reach the next mark. Lift needle out of fabric and clip thread.

Fig. 58

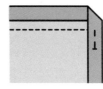

7. Repeat Steps 5 and 6 to continue sewing binding to quilt until binding overlaps beginning end by approximately 2". Trim excess binding.
8. If using $2^1/2$"w binding (finished size $1/2$"), trim backing and batting a scant $1/4$" larger than quilt top so that batting and backing will fill the binding when it is folded over to the quilt backing. If using narrower binding, trim backing and batting even with edges of quilt top.
9. On 1 edge of quilt, fold binding over to quilt backing and pin pressed edge in place, covering stitching line (**Fig. 59**). On adjacent side, fold binding over, forming a mitered corner (**Fig. 60**). Repeat to pin remainder of binding in place.

Fig. 59   **Fig. 60**

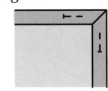

10. Blindstitch binding to backing, taking care not to stitch through to front of quilt.

ATTACHING BINDING WITH OVERLAPPED CORNERS

1. Matching raw edges and using a 1/4" seam allowance, sew a length of binding to top and bottom edges on right side of quilt.
2. If using 2 1/2"w binding (finished size 1/2"), trim backing and batting from top and bottom edges a scant 1/4" larger than quilt top so that batting and backing will fill the binding when it is folded over to the quilt backing. If using narrower binding, trim backing and batting even with edges of quilt top.
3. Trim ends of top and bottom binding even with edges of quilt top. Fold binding over to quilt backing and pin pressed edges in place, covering stitching line (**Fig. 61**); blindstitch binding to backing.

Fig. 61

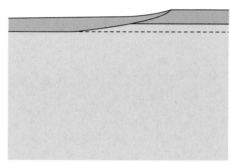

4. Leaving approximately 1 1/2" of binding at each end, stitch a length of binding to each side edge of quilt. Trim backing and batting as in Step 2.
5. Trim each end of binding 1/2" longer than bound edge. Fold each end of binding over to quilt backing (**Fig. 62**); pin in place. Fold binding over to quilt backing and blindstitch in place, taking care not to stitch through to front of quilt.

Fig. 62

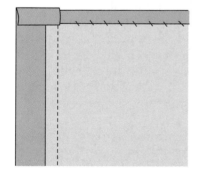

MAKING A HANGING SLEEVE

Attaching a hanging sleeve to the back of your wall hanging or quilt before the binding is added allows you to display your completed project on a wall.

1. Measure the width of the wall hanging top and subtract 1". Cut a piece of fabric 7"w by the determined measurement.
2. Press short edges of fabric piece 1/4" to wrong side; press edges 1/4" to wrong side again and machine stitch in place.
3. Matching wrong sides, fold piece in half lengthwise to form a tube.
4. Follow project instructions to sew binding to quilt top and to trim backing and batting. Before blindstitching binding to backing, match raw edges and stitch hanging sleeve to center top edge on back of wall hanging.
5. Finish binding wall hanging, treating the hanging sleeve as part of the backing.
6. Blindstitch bottom of hanging sleeve to backing, taking care not to stitch through to front of quilt.
7. Insert dowel or slat into hanging sleeve.

SIGNING AND DATING YOUR QUILT

Your completed quilt is a work of art and should be treated as such. And like any artist, you should sign and date your work. There are many different ways to do this, and you should pick a method of signing and dating that reflects the style of the quilt, the occasion for which it was made, and your own particular talents.

The following suggestions may give you an idea for recording the history of your quilt for future generations.

- Embroider your name, the date, and any additional information on the quilt top or backing. You may choose floss colors that closely match the fabric you are working on, such as white floss on a white border, or contrasting colors may be used.
- Make a label from muslin and use a permanent marker to write your information. Your label may be as plain or as fancy as you wish. Then stitch the label to the back of the quilt.
- Chart a cross-stitch label design that includes the information you wish and stitch it in colors that complement the quilt. Stitch the finished label to the quilt backing.

PILLOW FINISHING

Any quilt block may be made into a pillow. If desired, you may add welting to the pillow top before sewing the pillow top and back together.

ADDING WELTING TO PILLOW TOP

1. To make welting, use bias strip indicated in project instructions. (Or measure edges of pillow top and add 4". Measure circumference of cord and add 2". Cut a bias strip of fabric the determined measurement, piecing if necessary.)
2. Lay cord along center of bias strip on wrong side of fabric; fold strip over cord. Using a zipper foot, machine baste along length of strip close to cord. Trim seam allowance to the width you will use to sew pillow top and back together (see Step 2 of **Making the Pillow**).
3. Matching raw edges and beginning and ending 3" from ends of welting, baste welting to right side of pillow top. To make turning corners easier, clip seam allowance of welting at pillow top corners.
4. Remove approximately 3" of seam at 1 end of welting; fold fabric away from cord. Trim remaining end of welting so that cord ends meet exactly.

Fig. 63

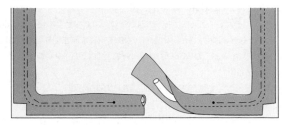

5. Fold short edge of welting fabric ½" to wrong side; fold fabric back over area where ends meet (**Fig. 64**).

Fig. 64

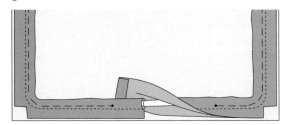

6. Baste remainder of welting to pillow top close to cord.

Fig. 65

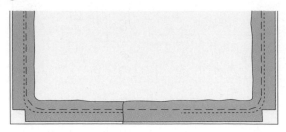

7. Follow **Making the Pillow** to complete pillow.

MAKING THE PILLOW

1. For pillow back, cut a piece of fabric the same size as pieced and quilted pillow top.
2. Place pillow back and pillow top right sides together. The seam allowance width you use will depend on the construction of the pillow top. If the pillow top has borders where the finished width of the border is not crucial, use a ½" seam allowance for durability. If the pillow top is pieced where a wider seam allowance would interfere with the design, use a ¼" seam allowance. Using the determined seam allowance (or stitching as close as possible to welting), sew pillow top and back together, leaving an opening at bottom edge for turning.
3. Turn pillow right side out, carefully pushing corners outward. Stuff with polyester fiberfill or pillow form and sew final closure by hand.

GLOSSARY

Appliqué — A cutout fabric shape that is secured to a larger background. Also refers to the technique of securing the cutout pieces.

Backing — The back or bottom layer of a quilt, sometimes called the "lining."

Backstitch — A reinforcing stitch taken at the beginning and end of a seam to secure stitches.

Basting — Large running stitches used to temporarily secure pieces or layers of fabric together. Basting is removed after permanent stitching.

Batting — The middle layer of a quilt that provides the insulation and warmth as well as the thickness.

Bias — The diagonal (45° for true bias) grain of fabric in relation to crosswise or lengthwise grain (see **Fig. 66**).

Binding — The fabric strip used to enclose the raw edges of the layered and quilted quilt. Also refers to the technique of finishing quilt edges in this way.

Blindstitch — A method of hand sewing an opening closed so that it is invisible.

Border — Strips of fabric that are used to frame a quilt top.

Chain piecing — A machine-piecing method consisting of joining pairs of pieces one after the other by feeding them through the sewing machine without cutting the thread between the pairs.

Grain — The direction of the threads in woven fabric. "Crosswise grain" refers to the threads running from selvage to selvage. "Lengthwise grain" refers to the threads running parallel to the selvages (**Fig. 66**).

Fig. 66

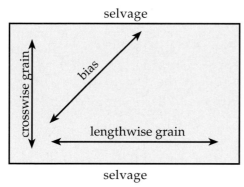

Machine baste — To baste using a sewing machine set at a long stitch length.

Miter — A method used to finish corners of quilt borders or bindings consisting of joining fabric pieces at a 45° angle.

Piecing — Sewing together the pieces of a quilt design to form a quilt block or an entire quilt top.

Pin basting — Using rust-proof safety pins to secure the layers of a quilt together prior to machine quilting.

Quilt block — Pieced or appliquéd sections that are sewn together to form a quilt top.

Quilt top — The decorative part of a quilt that is layered on top of the batting and backing.

Quilting — The stitching that holds together the 3 quilt layers (top, batting, and backing); or, the entire process of making a quilt.

Running stitch — A series of straight stitches with the stitch length equal to the space between stitches (**Fig. 67**).

Fig. 67

Sashing — Strips or blocks of fabric that separate individual blocks in a quilt top.

Seam allowance — The distance between the seam and the cut edge of the fabric. In quilting, the seam allowance is usually 1/4".

Selvages — The 2 finished lengthwise edges of fabric (see **Fig. 66**). Selvages should be trimmed from fabric before cutting.

Set (or Setting) — The arrangement of the quilt blocks as they are sewn together to form the quilt top.

Setting squares — Squares of plain (unpieced) fabric set between pieced or appliquéd quilt blocks in a quilt top.

Setting triangles — Triangles of fabric used around the outside of a diagonally-set quilt top to fill in between outer squares and border or binding.

Stencil — A pattern used for marking quilting lines.

Straight grain — The crosswise or lengthwise grain of fabric (see **Fig. 66**). The lengthwise grain has the least amount of stretch.

Strip set — Two or more strips of fabric that are sewn together along the long edges and then cut apart across the width of the sewn strips to create smaller units.

Template — A pattern used for marking quilt pieces to be cut out.

Triangle-square — In piecing, 2 right triangles joined along their long sides to form a square with a diagonal seam (**Fig. 68**).

Fig. 68

Unit — A pieced section that is made as individual steps in the quilt construction process are completed. Units are usually combined to make blocks or other sections of the quilt top.

CREDITS

We want to extend a warm *thank you* to the generous people who allowed us to photograph our projects at their homes.

- *Starry Log Cabin Collection:* Dr. Tony Johnson
- *Missouri Puzzle Collection:*
  Duncan and Nancy Porter
- *Prairie Stars:* Bill and Susan Roehrenbeck
- *Cake Stand Collection:*
  Duncan and Nancy Porter
- *Double Nine-Patch:* Duncan and Nancy Porter
- *Stars & Stripes Collection:*
  Carl and Monte Brunck
- *Fashion Fireworks:*
  Mr. and Mrs. James M. Adams
  and Duncan and Nancy Porter
- *Town Square:* Robert and Sheila West
- *Colonial Strippy Collection:*
  Bill and Susan Roehrenbeck
- *Aunt Lucinda's Chain:*
  Mr. and Mrs. Thomas Feurig
- *Centennial Medallion Collection:*
  Mr. and Mrs. James M. Adams
- *Tumbling Stars:* Mr. and Mrs. Thomas Feurig
- *Liberty Wall Quilts:*
  Duncan and Nancy Porter
- *Ohio Chain:* Mr. and Mrs. Thomas Feurig

The following projects were designed by Sharon LoMonaco: Stars & Stripes Collection, Starry Log Cabin Collection, Colonial Strippy Collection, Prairie Stars quilt, Ohio Chain quilt, and Missouri Puzzle quilt.

Thanks also go to Viking Husqvarna Sewing Machine Company of Cleveland, Ohio, for providing the sewing machines used to make many of the projects in this book.

To Magna IV Color Imaging of Little Rock, Arkansas, we say thank you for the superb color reproduction and excellent pre-press preparation.

We especially want to thank photographers Mark Mathews, Larry Pennington, Karen Shirey, and Ken West of Peerless Photography, Little Rock, Arkansas, and Jerry R. Davis of Jerry Davis Photography, Little Rock, Arkansas, for their time, patience, and excellent work.

We extend a sincere *thank you* to all the people who assisted in making and testing the projects in this book: Karen Call, Deborah B. Chance, Cindy Davis, Wanda Fite, Patricia Galas, Genny Garrett, Grace Grame, Judith H. Hassed, Judith M. Kline, Liz Lane, Barbara Middleton, Gazelle Mode, Ruby Solida, and Glenda Taylor; and members of the Gardner Memorial United Methodist Church, North Little Rock, Arkansas: Elois Allain, Maxie Bramblett, Leon Dickey, Vina Lendermon, Fredda McBride, Betty Smith, Esther Starkey, and Thelma Starkey.